OREGON ROAD TRIPS

MT. HOOD EDITION

WITH THE COLUMBIA RIVER GORGE

VIA THE MT. HOOD LOOP SCENIC BYWAY

MIKE & KRISTY WESTBY

ISBN-13: 978-0998395081

010124b – CS

Cover graphics by Sarah Craig – SarahCookDesign.com

DESCHUTES RIVER PRESS

"The whole mountain appeared as one glorious manifestation of divine power, enthusiastic and benevolent, glowing like a countenance with ineffable repose and beauty, before which we could only gaze in devout and lowly admiration."

John Muir - About Mt. Hood

FOLLOW DISCOVER-OREGON

11,245' Mt. Hood

On the Web:

www.Discover-Oregon.com

On Twitter:

@DiscoverOre.com

On Facebook:

www.Facebook.com/DiscoverORE

On Instagram:

DiscoverOregon4300

OREGON ROAD TRIPS - MT. HOOD EDITION

WITH THE COLUMBIA RIVER GORGE

Discover Mt. Hood & The Columbia River Gorge

An adventurous 3 to 5-day road trip exploring Mt. Hood and the Columbia River Gorge is now as easy as 1-2-3...

1) Write in the Dates of Your Trip
2) Make Your Historic Hotel Reservations
3) Pack Your Bags and Go!

Using this easy-to-use guide, you'll simply turn each page as you motor along and choose which points of interest to stop at and explore during your day's journey, *all while making your way toward an evening's stay at a historic Oregon hotel.*

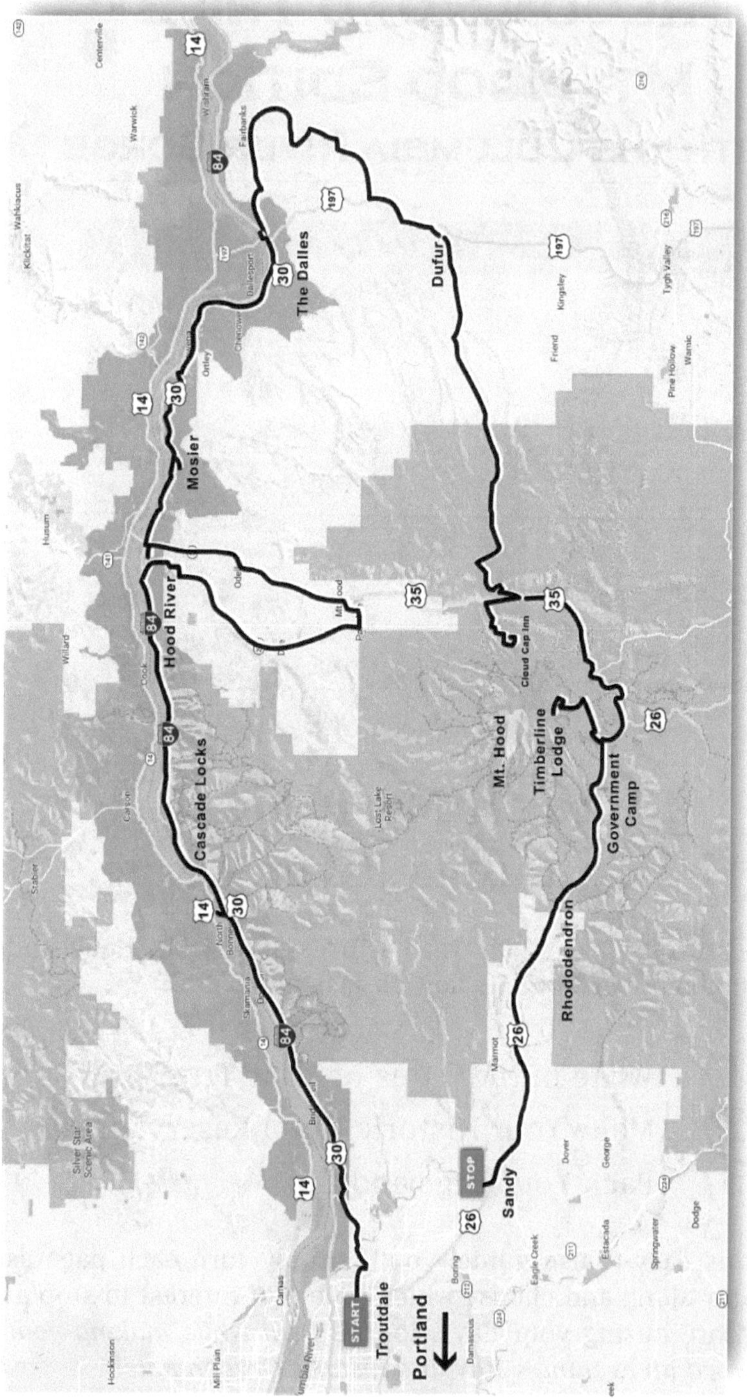
START
Troutdale
Portland
STOP
Sandy
Cascade Locks
Hood River
Mosier
The Dalles
Dufur
Cloud Cap Inn
Mt. Hood
Timberline Lodge
Government Camp
Rhododendron

TABLE OF CONTENTS

Your Journey

Additional Information

INTRODUCTION

Mt. Hood - Photo © Skibowl Adventure Park

Oregon is a vast and beautiful state. I could list its square mileage, its demographics or perhaps the distance from border to border, but a better description is...it starts with the shores of the Pacific Ocean on its western edge, traverses east over the Oregon Coast Range and into the verdant Willamette Valley, climbs over the snowy summits of the Cascade mountain range while skirting south of the sublime Columbia River Gorge and then continues forever into the remote, silent and dramatic beauty and history of far eastern Oregon.

This guide is about setting out on your own adventure to explore around Mt. Hood beginning with the majestic Columbia River Gorge. It's about the journey, not the destination. It's about asking, "I wonder where that goes?"...and going there. It's about opening a door and saying "Hello", walking into a place you've driven past far too many times, and standing at Timberline Lodge and imagining yourself triumphantly ascending to the lofty summit of Mt. Hood...and then making plans to do so. Enjoy your Oregon road trip around Mt. Hood!

How To Begin

The immense scope of Mt. Hood and the Columbia River Gorge can be too much to capture in one trip. In fact, its countless attractions can be so intimidating that travelers don't know where to begin...so they don't. Analysis paralysis.

Good news! This book already has your route planned for you. There are only three simple things you need to do...

1) Select the 3 to 5-day period for your trip and write those dates into this book at the beginning of each chapter.

2) Call and make reservations at the historic hotels found at the end of each day, which correspond with your chosen dates.

3) Pack your bags, hop in the car and simply choose the sights you wish to stop at and explore each day as you motor along. It's that easy!

Note that some of the optional activities you'll enjoy during your trip, such as flying in a historic biplane above Mt. Hood or riding aboard a sternwheeler on the Columbia River, will also require reservations, and these are noted at the beginning of each chapter/day.

Your Route

Your clockwise road trip around majestic Mt. Hood on the historic Mt. Hood Scenic Loop Highway "officially" begins in Troutdale, Oregon and takes you east out the Columbia River Gorge to Hood River for your first night, where you'll stay at the charming Columbia Gorge Hotel. You'll then spend the second day of your trip exploring a wonderful collection of attractions in this area before retiring for the evening at the Hood River Hotel. On Day 3, you'll continue making your way east out the Gorge to The Dalles, where you'll explore its local history and beautiful scenic destinations before arriving at the historic 1907 Balch Hotel in Dufur. Day 4 begins with a leisurely breakfast at the hotel before you begin your drive back west, ascending up through the forest toward Mt. Hood. Here, you'll drive a remote gravel road to the historic 1889 Cloud Cap Inn before setting out for the grand Timberline Lodge, situated at the 6,000' level on the south flank of the mountain. After a day of exploring around the lodge, taking in the amazing alpine views and perhaps enjoying a good book around the lodge's massive fireplace, you'll begin Day 5 with some exciting adventures and high-speed thrills in Government Camp, followed by setting out on a beautiful waterfall hike and exploring points along the historic Barlow Road. From there, you'll continue to Sandy, OR before beginning your trip home.

Timing

Your Mt. Hood and Columbia River Gorge road trip is a beautiful journey most anytime of the year, with the conditions changing dramatically from season to season. Spring, summer and fall "on the mountain" and "in the gorge" can bring some of the finest weather in Oregon, while winter can bring sunny mornings embraced by cool temperatures and wispy fog...or, quite often, treacherous icy conditions that can lock down travel for days. As a result, you'll want to be sure to check the weather forecast before leaving on your road trip.

WILDFLOWERS IN THE SPRINGTIME

If it is springtime and you like wildflowers, then you want to be in the Columbia River Gorge. Lupine, Chocolate Orchids, Penstemon, Indian Paintbrush, Howell's Daisy, Shooting Stars, Columbines and many others, including the dramatic Arrowleaf Balsamroot, cover the hillsides in an abundance of color. The wildflowers of the Columbia River Gorge do not bloom all at once, but instead over a period of about four months, usually mid-February through mid-June, with April and May offering the most vibrant displays. You'll find most of the wildflowers from the mid-gorge to out east, with locations such as the Mosier Plateau (Page 80), Tom McCall Point, Rowena Crest (Page 81) and many other sites offering outstanding experiences. At higher altitudes, near timberline on Mt. Hood, the wildflowers bloom later, with June and July bringing blossoming Bear Grass, Avalanche Lilies, Shooting Stars and more. While we list a couple of convenient wildflower spots in this guide, there are many more that are available with the aid of a short or long hike. If you are planning on visiting the area in the springtime, especially during April through July, we highly recommend you do an online search to learn more about the wildflowers of Mt. Hood and the Columbia River Gorge.

THE COLORS OF AUTUMN

Every fall, the deciduous trees of the Columbia River Gorge paint a scene of striking fall colors. The hillsides become accented with yellows, oranges, and vibrant reds as the leaves of Birches, Aspens, Willows, Poplars and Big Leaf Maples bid adieu to summer in a brilliant performance of autumn colors. It's Oregon's version of New England's fall colors, and you won't want to miss it if you are traveling here in late September and October.

Poison Oak (& Ticks and Snakes)

"Leaves of three, let it be!"

Don't let this stop you from enjoying a hike during your road trip, but be *very* mindful of poison oak when hiking in the Gorge, especially in the wooded areas at the eastern end. Just because you're on vacation doesn't mean it's taking a break from what it does best, and that is to cause a very itchy, blistering rash. Its deep green leaves cluster in groups of three, and the plant typically grows up to a few feet off the ground, so be mindful of small children, as it is right at their height. Its shiny leaves can be tempting for a child to grasp, but that shine is the oil that causes the rash, so don't touch it or brush against it with your clothes. Note that symptoms of a rash can take 12 hours to 10 days to appear.

In addition to Poison Oak, keep an eye out for ticks, especially if you have a dog, as well as any snakes. Most are harmless, but the rocky terrain of the eastern Gorge can harbor rattlesnakes, and these are highly venomous.

Add or Remove a Day to Customize Your Trip

This 3 to 5-day road trip around Mt. Hood can actually be any length you'd like. To shorten your trip, simply skip a night or two and combine the activities of a couple of days together. Want to lengthen your trip? Then by all means book another night at what will soon be your favorite new historic hotel and enjoy a leisurely extra day in your travels. For some additional ideas on how to make this a weekend road trip, see page 111.

Black & White Photos

So, what's up with the black and white photos instead of color? Well, we'd *really* like to use color photos throughout our guide. Seriously, that would be great! However, in order to reach economies of scale and keep the book affordable if we were to use color photos, we'd have to print thousands of copies at a time and probably store them on pallets in our garage. That's all well and fine, but it would mean that we couldn't make any updates to this guidebook until all of those copies were sold, which would take years. In order to regularly make updates, add new destinations, include more information, and even add additional photos, we use print-on-demand technology to print much smaller runs of books at a time. The only downside is that if we were to use color photos with POD technology, the costs involved with using color with these smaller print runs would make this guidebook prohibitively expensive, so the compromise is...black and white photos.

Some Ground Rules

"It's the Journey, Not the Destination."

The key to your journey is to alter your driving mindset. It really isn't about getting *there*, it's about discovering *here*. With this in mind, here are some ground rules to follow...

- Get used to stopping the car and getting out.
- Now stop the car and get out.
- Stop the car and get out...again. You'll be glad you did.
- Always ask "I wonder where that goes?"...and go there.
- Hit the brakes and turn right.
- Open the door and say "Hello."
- Don't assume it has to be a short conversation.
- Never mind that you just stopped back there...stop again here.
- Yes, it is a nice view. Feel free to stop, get out and admire it.
- This very moment is the time to do it. You won't be coming back this way next week.
- Enjoy the journey!

Travel Beyond the Page

By all means, do not feel you have to stop at only the places found in this book, as there are many more than those listed here just waiting to be discovered. Go ahead...follow that narrow lane, stop at that small museum, walk the trail to the viewpoint, and open the door to the shop that looks closed, but isn't. It's all about taking the time to...discover Oregon.

The Same, But Different

Following the information in this guide, you will enjoy a unique and exciting vacation discovering Mt. Hood and the Columbia River Gorge. It's important to note, however, that with a little creativity, you can also make this same journey a second or third time and have it be an almost entirely new and different trip each time. With trip number one, you may find you have only enough time in your day to explore Multnomah Falls, Hood River, and the Dufur Historical Museum, leaving the Mosier Tunnels, a trip to Cloud Cap Inn, and a flight in a historic biplane completely undiscovered. That means they'll all be waiting for you when you make your next trip!

"So, Where Are You From?"

There are many blessings on a trip like this, one of which is the number of conversations you simply fall into. It usually begins with a simple question or comment, and the next thing you know, you're involved in a 30-minute conversation with some of the nicest people you've ever met. Why? Because the folks you meet on a trip like this are your neighbors, it's just that they're a quite a few houses further down the block. If you approach a town, café, museum or someone with an air of traveling arrogance, then you're making a huge mistake. Instead, be genuine and friendly. You'll be amazed at how many people you'll meet and how pleasant your trip will be.

Get Some Good *Paper* Maps

We can't emphasize this enough. You will want to travel with and use a couple of good paper maps, and the more detailed, the better. Your phone will no doubt work well, but you're going to have the opportunity to explore some remote areas in this part of the state, some of which have no cell signal, so your phone will not work there. In addition, your paper maps will always boot up and never run out of power.

As you make your way along and stop at various locations, you'll often see folded Oregon maps made available for free by the Oregon Department of Transportation. These are very helpful, so grab more than one and keep them with you at all times. For more detail on the roads you'll be traveling, we also recommend the large Oregon atlases published by DeLorme. You can find them online for about $25.

Oregon's tourism division, Travel Oregon, also issues very helpful maps, magazines and trip guides. We highly recommend you visit their web site, www.TravelOregon.com, to order some of these free guides before setting out on your trip. Especially helpful is their large *Oregon Scenic Byways Official Driving Guide.*

If you are a member of AAA, check their resources, as well. By the way, make sure your membership is up-to-date.

Columbia River Gorge Parking Permits

The Columbia River Gorge is bordered by the state of Washington on its northern side, and the state of Oregon on its southern side. Each state requires a parking permit for the use of some of their more popular State Parks, Trail Heads, Scenic Areas, etc. As a result, travelers will need an Oregon State Parks permit for visiting sites on the Oregon side of the Columbia River Gorge, and a Washington Parks Discover Pass for visiting sites on the Washington side. If you are planning to return after this road trip and explore the entire Columbia River Gorge, you may purchase two annual permits, one for each state, or you may purchase daily permits at the sites you visit.

Oregon State Parks Day-Use Parking Permit - Daily: $5 - Annual: $30 - This permit is honored at all 26 Oregon State Parks that charge a parking fee. Permits are available at self-service kiosks, park booths, or offices located at the site in which a permit is required. In addition, they may be purchased by calling 800-551-6949 or online at https://www.oregonstateparks.org. Note that if you purchase a *daily* parking permit at one site in Oregon, you may use that permit at any other site in Oregon that requires the same permit *for the remainder of that day.* You do not need to buy a new permit at each site.

If you decide to hike any of the trails in the Gorge, note that 10 of the more popular trails require a parking pass, and this would need to be an Annual Northwest Forest Pass, a National Forest Recreation Day Pass, or an Interagency Annual, Senior or Access Pass.

Washington Parks Discover Pass - This permit is honored at over 100 Washington State Parks and recreation sites that charge a parking fee. Permits are available at self-service kiosks, licensed vendors, or offices located at the site in which a permit is required. In addition, they may be purchased by calling the number 866-320-9933 or online at https://www.discoverpass.wa.gov. Note that if you purchase a *daily* parking permit at one site in Washington, you may use that permit at any other site in Washington that requires the same permit *for the remainder of that day.* You do not need to buy a new permit at each site.

Online: https://www.discoverpass.wa.gov

- 1-Day Permit: $11.50
- Annual Permit: $35.00

At the Site:

- 1-Day Permit: $10.00 Cash
- Annual Permit: $30.00
  - Via credit card if a payment kiosk is available

BRING YOUR BINOCULARS

From dramatic waterfalls and lofty alpine glaciers to circling hawks and soaring bald eagles, there is much to see during your trip around Mt. Hood, so you may want to consider bringing a good pair of binoculars for use throughout your journey.

8 HOURS PER DAY – YOUR RESULTS MAY VARY

As we've mentioned, it's all about the journey and not the destination. That said, we found that after about 8 hours of being on the road, we were flipping this mantra and were ready to reach our destination. Our willingness to stop and explore was being replaced by a desire to simply reach our hotel, relax and "be there." Everybody's results will certainly vary, but we found that about 8 hours on the road was enough for a day.

Take Your Time and Enjoy the Sights

As you make your way through this book, you'll see a small clock icon placed next to some of the listings. There are many attractions that do not require much time to visit. A stop at the Vista House may require about half an hour, while a stop at Rowena Crest may require half that, but locations and attractions such as Multnomah Falls, the Mosier Tunnels, Cloud Cap Inn, and the Alpine Slide absolutely call for you to spend more time enjoying the commanding views or once-in-a-lifetime experiences. Wherever you see the clock icon, plan on spending at least an hour at that location, and we would encourage you to spend even more time there while hiking to a waterfall, exploring an interpretive center, or even riding aboard a sternwheeler. If it means missing out on some of the other stops, then so be it. They'll be waiting for you on your next trip around Mt. Hood!

The Historic Columbia River Highway

As you begin your journey through the Columbia River Gorge, you'll be traveling along the "King of Roads", the Historic Columbia River Highway. You will want to take a moment to read page 130 in this guide before you begin your road trip to learn more about this scenic Oregon icon and the amazing story behind it.

Make Your Reservations

Timberline Lodge

These are the reservations you will need to make for your trip. All necessary lodging reservations are shown in bold. All other listings are optional activities.

Day 1 - Troutdale, OR to Hood River, OR

Make a reservation for 1 night

- **The Columbia Gorge Hotel - 541-386-5566**
- The Columbia Gorge Hotel Spa - 541-387-8451
- Columbia Gorge Sternwheeler - 503-224-3900
- Heart of the Gorge Sailing - Sailboat - 941-400-0050

Day 2 - Explore Hood River, OR

Make a reservation for 1 night

- **The Hood River Hotel - 541-386-1900**
- Historic Biplane Flight - TacAero - 844-359-2827

Day 3 - Hood River, OR to Dufur, OR

Make a reservation for 1 night

- **The Balch Hotel - 541-467-2277**
- Tour of The Dalles Dam - Call 1 day in advance - 541-296-9778
- Nichols Art Glass - No reservation required - Just call to see if they are open today - 541-296-2143

Day 4 - Dufur, OR to Timberline Lodge

Make a reservation for 1 night

- **Timberline Lodge - 503-272-3311**
- Timberline Lodge Dining - Cascade Dining Room: 509-427-0202
- Cloud Cap Inn Tour - Summer Season - Hood River Ranger District - 541-352-6002
- Hike with the friendly St. Bernards of Timberline Lodge - 800-547-1406

Day 5 - Timberline Lodge to Sandy, OR and Going Home

- Mt. Hood Adventure Park at Skibowl - 503-272-3206

What Caused the Fire?

As you make your way along the western end of the Historic Columbia River Highway, you'll notice obvious signs of a large fire that swept through the area, as evidenced by swaths of trees with blackened trunks, chainsawed stumps, and silver tree snags covering nearby hillsides and distant ridges.

In September of 2017, someone carelessly tossed a lit firework into dry grass and leaves while hiking in the Columbia River Gorge, and this set off a massive wildfire that burned for weeks, closed I-84 for an extended period, forced the evacuation of hundreds of people from their homes, destroyed many historic trails and structures in the Gorge, and consumed nearly 50,000 acres of forest land. Thankfully, only 15% of that area was rated as "Highly Burned".

Thanks to the brave efforts of hardworking firefighters and emergency responders, as well as countless volunteers and the citizens of communities throughout the Columbia River Gorge, most of the Gorge was saved from this devastating wildfire, and today trails are being reopened, bridges are being rebuilt, and the burned areas are again springing to life.

Day One

The Historic Columbia River Highway Scenic Byway

Troutdale to Hood River

Crown Point Vista House - Historic Columbia River Highway

DAY 1
TROUTDALE TO HOOD RIVER

Day 1 - Date: / /

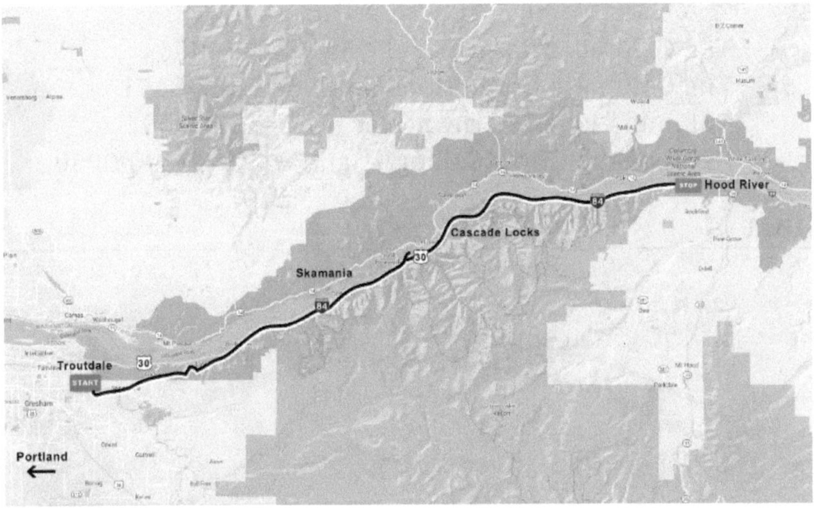

Summary: Where You're Going Today:

- Troutdale, OR
- Historic Columbia River Highway
- Columbia River Gorge Waterfalls
- Cascade Locks, OR
- Hood River, OR

Today's route travels the Historic Columbia River Highway along the northern border of Oregon, taking you from Troutdale to the Crown Point Vista House, which offers a stunning and iconic view of the Columbia River Gorge from its western end. From there, you'll motor through history as you visit a series of graceful waterfalls on your way to the massive Bonneville Dam, where you'll witness the power of the mighty Columbia River. Afterwards, you'll explore the small town of Cascade Locks before arriving at your destination for the evening, the historic Columbia Gorge Hotel in Hood River.

Tonight's Lodging:

- The Columbia Gorge Hotel & Spa

Today's Mileage: 50 Miles

Reservations Needed for This Segment:

- The Columbia Gorge Hotel - 541-386-5566
- The Columbia Gorge Hotel Spa - 541-387-8451
- Columbia River Sternwheeler - 503-224-3900
- Heart of the Gorge Sailing - Sailboat - 941-400-0050

Start

Your Mt. Hood Road Trip begins at the west end of the Columbia River Gorge, in the town of Troutdale. To get there...

- Travel I-84 East from Portland and take Exit 17.

- Continue straight from the exit for 0.7 mile to Graham Road. Turn right here and follow this south for 0.3 mile to the Columbia River Highway / Historic Route 30. Turn left / east here, where you'll then pass under the large "Gateway to the Gorge" sign.

- You are now on the Historic Columbia River Highway Scenic Byway and beginning your road trip around Mt. Hood via the Columbia River Gorge. Note that the small shops and restaurants you're passing here in Troutdale make for an excellent stop for breakfast or to grab a cup of coffee.

The Columbia River Gorge

The Columbia River Gorge is a natural wonder of sublime grandeur filled with elegant and majestic waterfalls, towering geological features, endless vistas, and fields of colorful spring wildflowers that bloom from mid-February through June, and then dry in the summer winds before welcoming autumn's fiery oranges, reds and yellows.

In addition, it is an area rich in ancient and modern history. At one time, thousands of Native Americans from around the west would gather annually near Celilo Falls to engage in trade of all forms, as well as renew old friendships. Lewis and Clark journeyed down the Columbia in 1806 on their way to the Pacific, and the pioneers of the Oregon Trail faced the last big test of their journey by braving the dangerous and unforgiving rapids of the Cascades.

☐ **Your First Stop:** Rail Depot Museum - Depot Park

Railroads have played a very important role in Oregon's history, and their history in the Gorge runs back to before the turn of the 20th century. In fact, later today in Cascade Locks, you'll see the Oregon Pony, the very first steam locomotive used in the Oregon Territory. For now, you'll visit Troutdale's Rail Depot Museum. Originally built in 1882 and rebuilt in 1907 after it burned, the museum offers visitors a look at just how the depot appeared when it was in use in the early 1900s. In addition, rail fans will find a nicely restored Union Pacific caboose in the parking lot.

Rail Depot Museum / Gateway to the Gorge Visitor Center
473 E. Historic Columbia River Highway
Troutdale, OR 97060
503-661-2164

- Open: Every Friday from 10:00 a.m. to 2:00 p.m.

Driving Directions: From the "Gateway to the Gorge" sign, travel east for 0.2 miles, where you'll find the entrance to the museum on your left.

☐ **Next Stop:** Harlow House Museum & Park

Built in 1900, the Harlow House showcases the lifestyle, furnishings and belongings of families in the area at the turn of the 20th century. In addition, visitors will find changing exhibits, photos, artwork, and a short interpretive pathway outside.

Harlow House Museum & Park
762 E. Historic Columbia River Highway
Troutdale, OR 97060
503-661-2164

- Open: Sunday - 1:00 p.m. to 3:00 p.m.

Driving Directions: From the Rail Depot Museum, continue along the Columbia River Highway for 0.2 miles to the Harlow House on your right.

☐ **Next Stop:** Barn Exhibit Hall

The large Barn Exhibit Hall features changing exhibits, which tell of the rich history of Troutdale and the surrounding area. Currently, visitors will find an impressively curated exhibit marking the 100th anniversary of the Historic Columbia River Highway, the first highway in the United States to be built as a scenic road, as well as the first to include a painted center line!

Barn Exhibit Hall
732 E. Historic Columbia River Highway
Troutdale, OR 97060
503-661-2164

- Open: Wednesday through Saturday - 10:00 a.m. to 3:00 p.m., Sunday - 1:00 p.m. to 3:00 p.m.

Driving Directions: The Barn Exhibit Hall is located next door to the Harlow House Museum & Park.

☐ **Next Stop:** Women's Forum Overlook

From 1912 to 1930, this spot was home to the Chanticleer Inn. Known for its famous chicken dinners, it was *the* place for the Portland elite to gather when setting out on an adventure beyond Portland. However, getting here was quite the chore, as travelers would have to journey 25 miles by train or boat to the base of the cliff below and then walk or shuttle by horse-drawn wagon up a steep dirt road to the inn. (You can find remnants of the old road as it disappears into the woods at the north end of the parking lot) Like so many buildings of this era, the Chanticleer Inn burned down, on October 8th, 1930. (Photo Circa 1916)

Today, the Women's Forum Overlook is a tribute to the founding members of the Portland Women's Forum, who worked tirelessly to raise the funds necessary to buy this point and preserve its amazing view for future generations.

Driving Directions: From the Barn Exhibit Hall, continue on the Columbia River Highway for 0.4 miles, where you'll take a right turn after crossing a large narrow bridge over the Sandy River. Continue from here for 8.3 miles to the Woman's Forum Overlook on your left.

☐ **Next Stop:** Crown Point Vista House

Offering a commanding view into the heart of the Columbia River Gorge at the west end of the old Columbia River Highway, the Crown Point Vista House is one of Oregon's classic historical icons. Built atop a massive basalt promontory in 1917, its unique stone structure is "a temple to the natural beauty of the Gorge." Inside, travelers will find a museum showcasing the history of the building and the Columbia River Gorge, as well as a small gift shop, restrooms, and a café serving coffee.

Crown Point Vista House
40700 E. Columbia River Highway
Corbett, OR 97019
503-344-1368

- Open Daily: 9:00 a.m. - 4:00 p.m.
- Closed if winds exceed 50 mph or if there is snow or ice.

Driving Directions: From the Woman's Forum Overlook, continue east on the Historic Columbia River Highway for 1.2 miles to the Crown Point Vista House.

Note that at the 0.4 mile mark you'll see East Larch Mountain Road veering off to the right, heading to Larch Mountain. This destination is not on today's journey, but if you were to come this way again and follow this road for 14 miles up to the "summit" of Larch Mountain, you'd find a large paved parking area with a path leading to a viewpoint offering an amazing "reach out and touch it" view of Mt. Hood, as well as views of Mt. Rainier, Mt. St. Helens, Mt. Adams and in the distance, Mt. Jefferson. Note that East Larch Mountain Road is closed with a gate 10 miles up the road from late fall to early spring. It is also a popular road with cyclists, so be sure to keep a careful eye out for them as you drive to the summit and back.

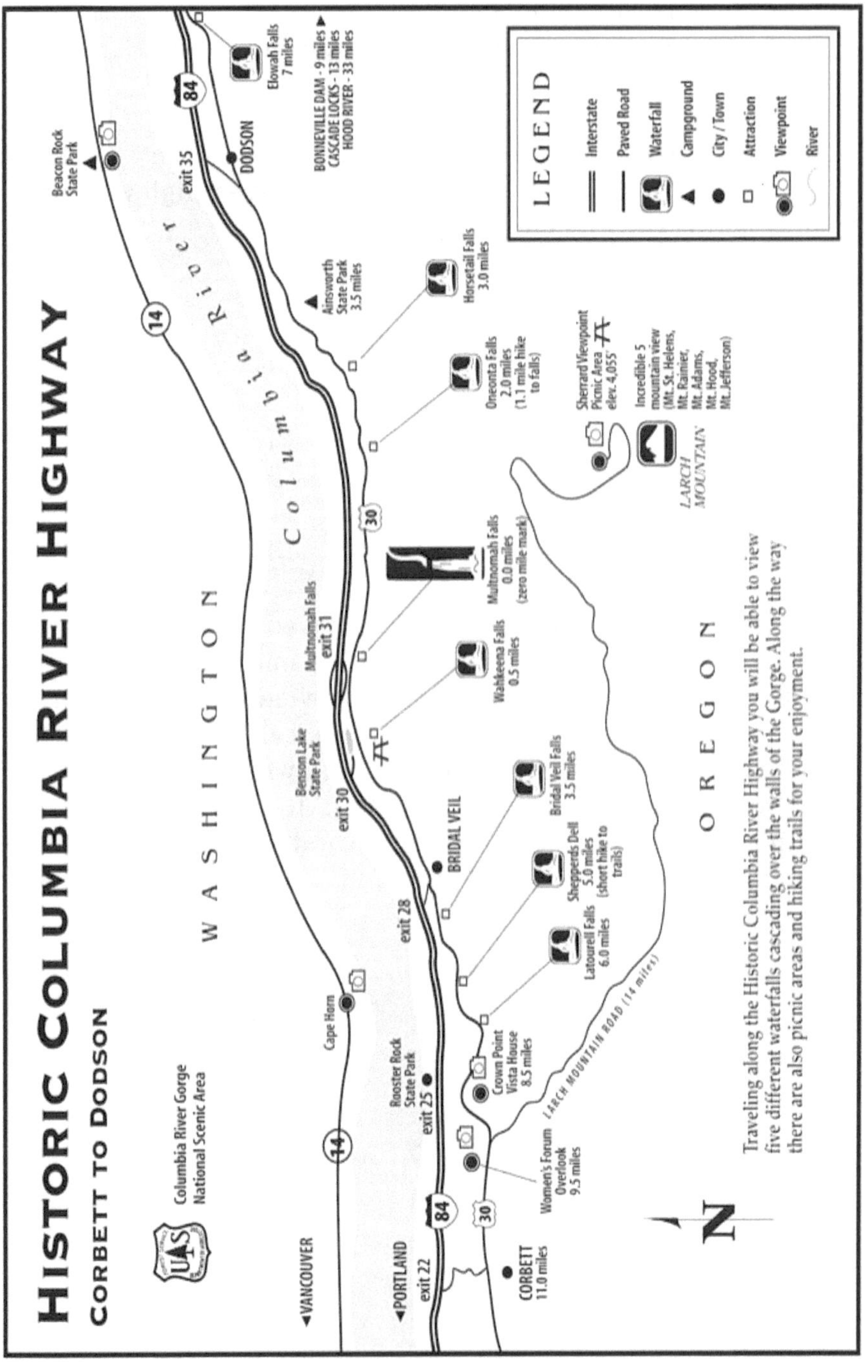

Map courtesy of Friends of Multnomah Falls

COLUMBIA RIVER GORGE WATERFALLS

The Columbia River Gorge is home to over two dozen beautiful waterfalls close to the highway, with Multnomah Falls being by far the most popular. Appearing one after the other as you motor along, stop and visit any one of them along this stretch of the Historic Columbia River Highway. Many, such as Latourell Falls, have short hikes with a great view.

Appearing in order as you drive east:

- Latourell Falls
- Shepperd's Dell
- Bridal Veil Falls
- Wahkeena Falls
- Multnomah Falls
- Oneonta Falls
- Horsetail Falls
- Elowah Falls

THE WATERFALL CORRIDOR

To enter the Waterfall Corridor, drive east from the Crown Point Vista House (Page 30) along the Historic Columbia River Highway and stop at any of the waterfalls you find along the way, which are listed in their order of appearance on the following pages.

☐ **Next Stop:** Latourell Falls

Introduce yourself to the waterfalls of the Columbia River Gorge with beautiful Latourell Falls. Featuring an amphitheatre with striking columnar basalt and a large yellow patch of lichen, Latourell Falls drops uninterrupted for 224 feet, often in a thin stream, before disappearing into a pool below. Follow the stairs from the parking lot, which take you up to a trail that leads to a viewpoint only a short distance away, or opt to take a slightly descending path from the west side of the parking area, near the road, to the base of the falls.

Once at the falls, cross a small foot bridge and follow the paved path only a short distance further to see an amazing example of the Arch Deck Bridge design employed by Sam Hill and Samuel Lancaster when building the Historic Columbia River Highway.

☐ **Next Stop:** Shepperd's Dell Falls

Named after George Shepperd, the land owner who presented the falls and its accompanying 11 acre parcel to the City of Portland in May of 1915, Shepperd's Dell Falls drops over 90 feet in a two-tiered display before making its way under a classic 1914 deck arch bridge, a captivating example of the impressive engineering employed with the Historic Columbia River Highway. Find the beginning of the short paved path to the falls down a small flight of stairs, near the east end of the bridge.

☐ **Next Stop:** Bridal Veil Falls

You have your choice of two paths at Bridal Veil Falls. One leads to sweeping vistas of the Columbia River Gorge, while the other takes you to a viewing platform opposite the falls.

Make your way to the east end of the parking lot and find a trail that splits near the restrooms. The paved path to the left takes you on a short interpretive loop that leads to a collection of viewpoints high on a bluff overlooking the Columbia River. Choose the path that veers to the right, and you'll soon drop down into the forest along a gravel path that traverses a set of switchbacks, small bridges and concrete steps before leading up to a viewing platform across from Bridal Veil Falls. It's about ¼ mile, at best. Note that you'll want to be mindful of the Poison Oak in this area.

Next Stop: Wahkeena Falls

A short 0.2 mile hike along a paved path takes you up to a historic hand-crafted stone bridge fronting Wahkeena Falls. Dropping as a fall and then a cascade for over 240 feet, it is one of the more photogenic falls you'll find in the Columbia River Gorge. Note that the bridge can become heavily ice encrusted and very treacherous when temperatures reach below freezing.

Next Stop: Multnomah Falls

As you make your way through the list of waterfalls, you'll come upon majestic Multnomah Falls. Falling in two stages, separated by the historic Benson Bridge, Multnomah Falls towers at 620 feet high, making it the tallest waterfall in all of Oregon and creating such an impressive site that it draws more than 2 million visitors every year. In fact, it is the most visited natural recreation site in the Pacific Northwest.

The walk from the often busy parking area to the falls is very short, and the option exists to hike up to the Benson Bridge or to continue on all the way up to a viewing platform at the crest of the upper falls for a unique and memorable view. (1.2 Miles)

Multnomah Falls Lodge, built in 1925, offers a Visitor Center, gift shop, a snack bar, and a restaurant, which serves breakfast at 8:00 a.m., lunch at 11:00 a.m., and dinner at 4:00 p.m.

- Open: Multnomah Falls is open year-round, and the Visitor Center is open daily from 9:00 a.m. to 5:00 p.m.

Driving Directions: You'll come upon Multnomah Falls as you make your way east along the Historic Columbia River Highway. *After visiting Multnomah Falls*, you'll continue on to Oneonta Falls, Horsetail Falls and Elowah Falls. To do so, travel east from Multnomah Falls on the Historic Columbia River Scenic Byway for 3.6 miles to where you take the road to the right for *Hood River - I-84 - Route 30 East.* Take this and continue a little over 0.2 miles to where you turn right onto Frontage Road *instead of taking the onramp to I-84 Eastbound on the left.* (Note that it is OK if you do get onto I-84 here, you'll just miss Elowah Falls.) Continue on Frontage Road until you join I-84 just after passing the trailhead for Elowah Falls. Continue on I-84 East until taking *Exit 40 - Bonneville Dam*, in just under three miles.

☐ **Next Stop:** Oneonta Falls

A unique Columbia River Gorge adventure. In addition to offering hiking trails to Lower, Middle, and Upper Oneonta Falls, visitors may also climb over a large log jam and wade through Oneonta Creek up Oneonta Canyon to the base of Oneonta Falls. It's a popular hike, though most folks wait until the water level is low, since the water can be a tad cool!

Note: Due to the fire of 2017, all of the trails to Oneonta Falls are closed for an indefinite period of time.

☐ **Next Stop:** Horsetail Falls

Located right next to the Historic Columbia River Highway, graceful Horsetail Falls drops as a flowing ribbon for a full 176 feet before dispersing into a large pool at its base. Park and walk across the highway to a nearby observation area at the base of the falls. Note that the parking area on your left can come up kind of quickly, but there is a second entrance a little further along the highway.

☐ **Next Stop:** Elowah Falls

Plunging over a dramatic cliff face and free-falling for over 200 feet, Elowah Falls rewards those who make the easy 0.8 mile hike to its base with a captivating picturesque scene. A striking basalt amphitheatre offering scattered patches of bright yellow and green lichen forms the backdrop as the water falls and disperses below before disappearing amidst mossy boulders as McCord Creek.

Note: Car break-ins in the Waterfall Corridor are a chronic problem. If you stop to admire the waterfalls and enjoy some of the short hikes, DO NOT leave valuables inside your car, nor leave bags which appear tempting within sight. Yes, you know there's nothing in that backpack, but thieves found a wallet in the last one they stole, so they'll take yours just to see what's inside. In addition, do not arrive, get out and put valuables, such as a purse or a pack, into your trunk and walk away. There is a history of thieves watching for this kind of activity so as to learn what you have and where it is stored. Because of its quick access to I-84, break-ins occur throughout this area, but especially in the Multnomah Falls and Oneonta Gorge parking lots.

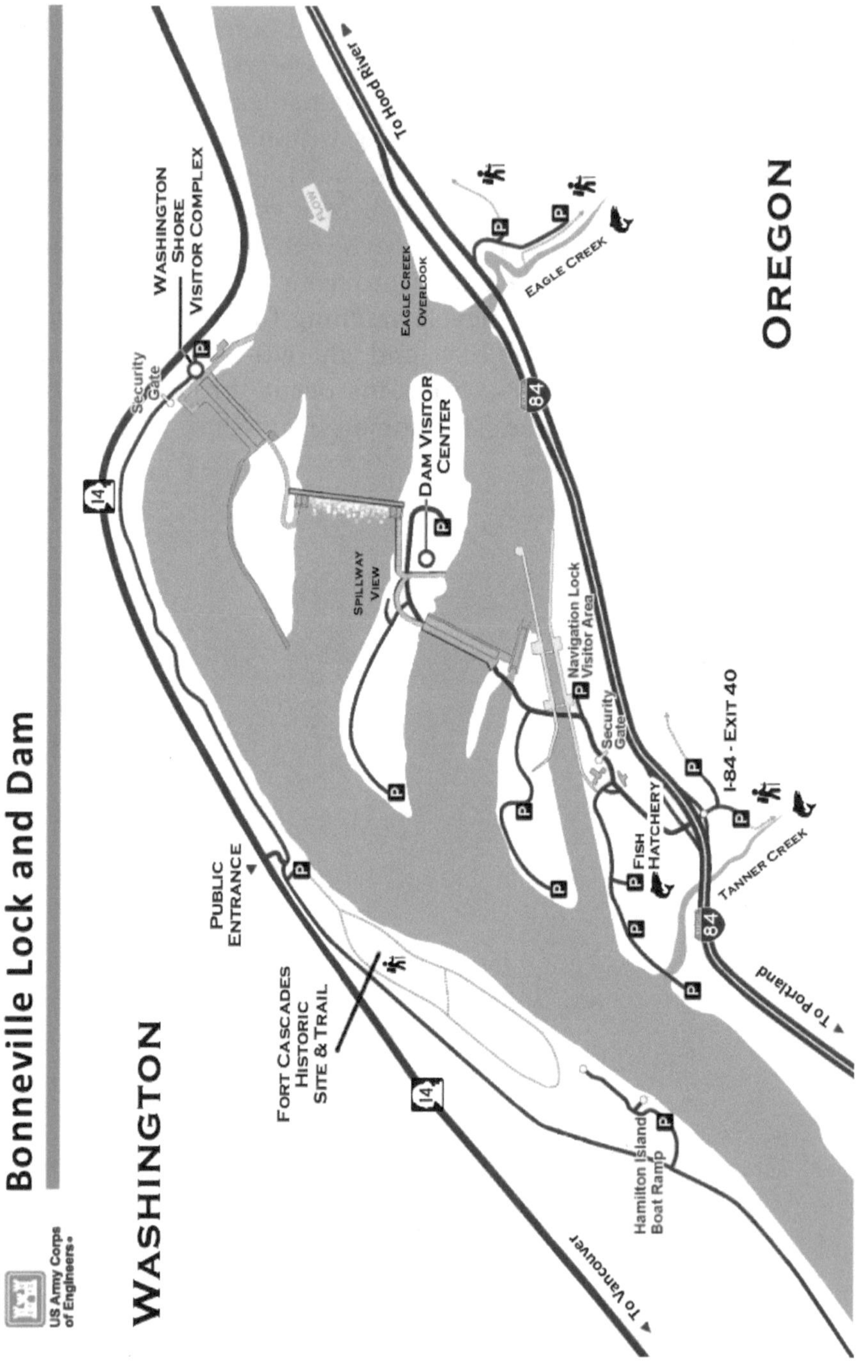

US Army Corps of Engineers
Bonneville Lock and Dam
WASHINGTON
OREGON
Washington Shore Visitor Complex
Security Gate
Eagle Creek Overlook
Dam Visitor Center
Spillway View
Navigation Lock Visitor Area
Security Gate
Fish Hatchery
I-84 - Exit 40
Eagle Creek
Tanner Creek
Public Entrance
Fort Cascades Historic Site & Trail
Hamilton Island Boat Ramp
To Hood River
To Portland
To Vancouver
FLOW
14
84

BONNEVILLE LOCK & DAM

As you make your way deep into the Columbia River Gorge, you'll find yourself at the Bonneville Lock & Dam. Built in 1934 by the US Corps of Engineers with funding from the Works Progress Administration, the dam provided thousands of jobs for those who were out of work because of the Great Depression. Today, in addition to providing safe passage for river vessels, it captures the mighty Columbia and harnesses its power for use in a myriad ways throughout the Pacific Northwest and beyond.

☐ **Next Stop:** The Locks at the Bonneville Dam

It's not everyday that you get to see vessels large and small up close as they pass through a large river lock...well, unless you work at the locks of Bonneville Dam! On your way to visiting the Bonneville Lock & Dam Visitor Center, take the first right after passing through the guard shack, park, and then walk over to the railing to get a sense of vertigo as you peer down into the locks holding back the river with their massive gates. Hopefully, your timing will be good and a ship will be passing through while you're there. If not, don't bother asking when one will be arriving next, as the lock tenders do not have any of that information. When a ship shows up, they simply work the gates to allow it to pass before waiting for the next ship to arrive.

Driving Directions: Take Exit 40 from I-84 East - Turn left at the stop and proceed under I-84 onto NE Bonneville Way. Continue until you are required to stop at the armed security checkpoint. Once waived on, take the first right open to the public, which leads to a parking area for the locks.

☐ **Next Stop:** Bonneville Dam Fish Viewing Window / Bonneville Lock & Dam Visitor Center

Here's an opportunity to get a fascinating up close look at the migrating salmon of the Columbia River. Stop by the Bonneville Lock & Dam Visitor Center and follow the signs to the elevators that will take you downstairs to the fish viewing windows. There, depending upon the time of year, you'll see countless migrating Chinook, Sockeye, or Coho salmon, as well as steelhead, shad, and even the strange looking lamprey swimming their way upriver past the window. The key, however, is understanding when the fish runs are occurring, otherwise you'll stop by and see nothing but empty water flowing past. Check the *Average Monthly Fish Count Chart* on page 129 to see both when and what kind of fish will be swimming past the fish viewing window, or call the Fish Count Hotline beforehand to check if any salmon are currently migrating upriver. Fish runs in the spring, as well as late August through October, peaking in September, provide plenty of fish to see. Note that if the fish are not running, the Visitor Center is still worth a visit.

- Check the *Average Monthly Fish Count Chart* on page 129 to see if fish may be running during your visit.
- Bonneville Dam Interpretive Center: 541-374-8820
- Fish Count Hotline: 541-374-4011

Driving Directions: From the Bonneville Dam locks, proceed northward across the face of the dam to the large parking lot on the east side of the Visitor Center. Directions to the Fish Viewing Window are clearly displayed inside the center.

☐ **Next Stop:** A Better View of the Dam

You'll have a pretty good view of the Bonneville Dam while at the Visitor Center, but for an even better and closer view, turn right onto Dam Road shortly after leaving the Visitor Center, then turn right again and you'll see two parking areas on your left which offer an unobstructed view of the dam, hopefully with the water flowing through in an impressive display of force.

☐ **Next Stop:** Bonneville Dam Hatchery

Open to the public year-round, the Bonneville Hatchery at the Bonneville Lock & Dam has display ponds holding thousands of trout and salmon fry, as well as sturgeon. Make your way to the small Sturgeon Viewing and Interpretive Center behind the hatchery building and step inside to see *huge* sturgeon and salmon swimming past the large viewing window. It is here that you'll

see Herman, an adult White Sturgeon measuring more than 10' in length! Also, be sure to see the nearby Trout Pond, where the 18" trout are small in comparison to the others. Be sure to have a quarter in hand so you can buy food to feed the fish!

Bonneville Fish Hatchery

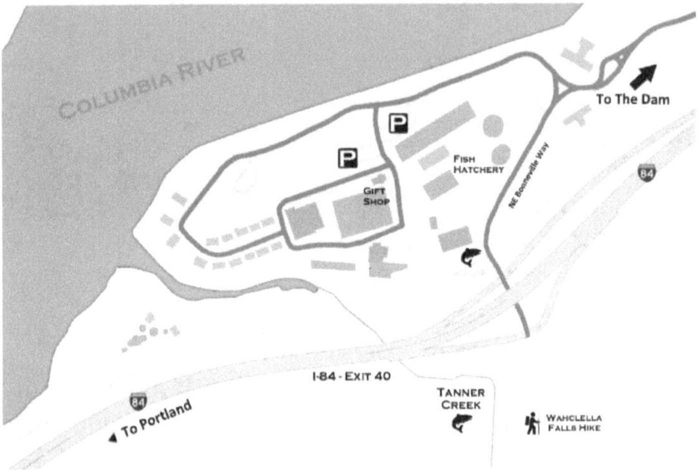

Bonneville Dam Hatchery
70543 NE Herman Loop
Cascade Locks, OR 97014
541-374-8393

- Located west of the Bonneville Dam

Driving Directions: Take Exit 40 from I-84 East and turn left to proceed under I-84 onto NE Bonneville Way. In a short distance, turn left onto NE Sturgeon Ln. and park near the gift shop. Then walk over to the hatchery.

If you are coming here from the Bonneville Dam Fish Viewing Window, (Page 42) or view of the dam, (Page 43) look for signs to the hatchery / NE Sturgeon Ln. as you begin to leave the Dam area and approach I-84.

☐ **Next Stop:** Spawning Salmon (Sept. & Oct.)

During the last days of August, as well as the months of September and October, visitors to the Bonneville Lock & Dam area can see spawning salmon in nearby Tanner Creek.

Driving Directions: Exit I-84 at Exit 40, but instead of turning left and passing under I-84 to Bonneville Dam, turn right and park at the Wahclella Falls trailhead. (Which is an excellent 2-mile round trip triple-falls hike, by the way.) Walk over to the nearby Tanner Creek to see the salmon. Note that a parking permit, such as a Northwest Forest Pass, is required here.

☐ **Next Stop:** Cascade Salmon Hatchery

Located next to the trailhead of the popular Eagle Creek Trail is the Cascade Salmon Hatchery. Open year-round, the hatchery focuses on egg incubation and the rearing of Coho salmon, so there's a good chance you'll see its rearing ponds full of small salmon fingerlings when you stop by. Note that large adult Coho and Chinook salmon return to spawn in the nearby Eagle Creek during the months of September and October, and this can be quite the spectacle of nature to observe.

Cascade Salmon Hatchery
74152 NE Eagle Creek Loop
Cascade Locks, OR 97014
541-374-8381

- Open: 7:30 a.m. to 4:30 p.m., though visitors can walk around the rearing ponds after hours. Personnel are more than happy to answer any questions visitors may have while the hatchery is open.

Note: A parking permit is not needed when parking *at the hatchery*. If you park near the busy Eagle Creek Trail trailhead just to the south, then you will need an Annual Northwest Forest Pass, a National Forest Recreation Day Pass, or an Interagency Annual, Senior or Access Pass.

Driving Directions: From the Bonneville Dam, continue east on I-84 for a little over 1 mile to *Exit 41 - Fish Hatchery - Eagle Creek Rec Area.* (Note: The exit occurs shortly after exiting a tunnel, so you may wish to be in the right lane when entering the tunnel.) The salmon hatchery is directly in front of you when you stop at the end of the exit. Do not leave valuables in your car if you park near the Eagle Creek Trailhead.

☐ **Next Stop:** Eagle Creek Overlook

Built in 1937 by the Civilian Conservation Corp, the Eagle Creek Overlook gave sightseers a place from which to watch the construction of the massive Bonneville Dam. Today, it gives travelers a captivating view of the dam and the river that's a little bit off the beaten path and well worth the stop.

Driving Directions: To the north of the Cascade Salmon Hatchery is the onramp you will soon take for I-84 Eastbound to Cascade Locks. However, to the left of the start of the onramp is a two lane road (#243) that leads west, under I-84 and to the Eagle Creek Overlook. Take this road and follow it to the parking area, where you'll find a short trail leading north to the overlook. Note that the stretch of Eagle Creek next to the road leading west is an excellent spot to see migrating salmon during September and October.

Cascade Locks

Cascade Locks welcomes visitors with a growing collection of restaurants, a wealth of adventures, and a fascinating story that reveals the history of the indigenous people of the area, the courage of the Oregon Trail pioneers, and the powerful geologic, hydraulic and volcanic forces that shaped the gorge.

Driving Directions: From the Cascade Salmon Hatchery and Eagle Creek Overlook, take the onramp to I-84 Eastbound and continue east to *Exit 44 - Cascade Locks - Stevenson.* This exit rolls you right onto the main drag in town, Wa Na Pa Street.

Note: When you leave Cascade Locks, you will travel over I-84 and take a backroad east, rejoining I-84 Eastbound at Exit 51.

Cascade Locks Stop: Eastwind Drive-In

The place to hit after a day of adventure in the Columbia River Gorge, the Eastwind Drive-In offers burgers, fries, shakes and the largest chocolate & vanilla swirl soft-serve ice cream cone you'll ever see in your life! Simply continue down the main drag of Cascade Locks after getting off I-84 and you'll see it on the left.

Eastwind Drive-In
395 NW Wa Na Pa Street
Cascade Locks, OR 97014
541-374-8380

Cascade Locks Stop: Brigham Fish Market

If you'd prefer some delicious seafood, including halibut, shrimp, clams and oysters, as well as freshly caught Columbia River salmon and sturgeon, all prepared in a variety of ways, including Gluten Free, then stop in at one of our favorite Cascade Locks restaurants, Brigham Fish Market. Grab a table inside or enjoy outdoor seating in the sun.

Brigham Fish Market
681 Wa Na Pa Street
Cascade Locks, OR 97014
541-374-9340

Open:

- Monday and Tuesday - 11:00 a.m. to 6:00 p.m.
- Thursday through Sunday - 10:00 a.m. to 6:00 p.m.
- Closed Wednesdays

☐ **Cascade Locks Stop:** Thirsty Coffee Bar

Does your road trip need a flavorful coffee, hot chocolate, iced tea, smoothie, breakfast sandwich, pastry or ??? Then stop in at Thirsty Coffee Bar and enjoy their locally made offerings. Oh, and be sure to ask about The Joy Foundation.

Thirsty Coffee Bar
504 Wa Na Pa Street
Cascade Locks, OR 97014

- Open Monday through Saturday - 6:00 a.m. to 6:00 p.m., Sundays - 7:00 a.m. to 6:00 p.m.

☐ **Cascade Locks Stop:** Historical Museum

Built in 1905, the museum provides guests with a look at the history of the Cascade Locks area through displays, photos and artifacts. Outside, in its own climate controlled building, is The Oregon Pony, the first steam locomotive ever used in Oregon.

Cascade Locks Historical Museum
SW Portage Rd.
Cascade Locks, OR 97014
541-374-8535

- Open May - September - 12:00 p.m. - 5:00 p.m. - $4
- Closed Mondays, except holidays

Driving Directions: Heading east on Wa Na Pa Street, take the first left after the Eastwind Drive-In onto SW Portage Road and follow this to the Port of Cascade Locks Marine Park. Take the first left after passing underneath the railroad tracks.

☐ **Cascade Locks Stop:** Thunder Island

After visiting the museum, take a moment to walk across the locks, which were built over 120 years ago, in 1896, and explore the park-like setting of Thunder Island. It's an excellent way to see the locks up close, and the far shore provides a beautiful view of the river, as well as a great place to enjoy lunch from the Eastwind Drive-In or Brigham Fish Market.

Walking Directions: From the Historical Museum, walk north to the foot bridge over the locks to Thunder Island.

☐ **Cascade Locks Stop:** Columbia Gorge Sternwheeler Cruise

See the Columbia River Gorge from "the best view on the Columbia" during a one or two hour sightseeing and interpretive cruise aboard the historic Columbia Gorge Sternwheeler. Approximately three cruises per day in the summer. Call 503-224-3900 to book your cruise.

Columbia Gorge Sternwheeler
299 SW Portage Rd.
Cascade Locks, OR 97014
541-374-8427

Driving Directions: From the Historical Museum, drive back east along SW Portage Road to the 4-way intersection by the railroad tracks, but instead of turning right to pass back underneath the tracks, proceed straight. Drive 1/8 mile to the Visitor Center and Locks Waterfront Café, located in the Cascade Locks Marine Park. Note that the Locks Waterfront Café here is open from 10:30 a.m. - 6:00 p.m. daily, May to October. 541-645-0372

☐ **Cascade Locks Stop:** Set Sail on the Columbia River

As an option to cruising aboard the Columbia Gorge Sternwheeler, consider setting sail on the mighty Columbia! It's easy to do...simply make a reservation *at least* two hours in advance online or by phone, meet your hosts, Preston and Chennie, at the Cascade Locks Marina, and then board their beautiful 38' sloop "Wy'East" for a two hour sailing adventure. Choose to help sail the boat or just sit back and enjoy the view. Sunset sails are also available and they are especially beautiful in this part of the gorge.

You'll find the Wy'East docked in the marina immediately east of where you board the Columbia Gorge Sternwheeler. Note that Wy'East holds two to six passengers. Visit their web site for additional details and to make a reservation.

Heart of the Gorge Sailing
Cascade Locks Marina
Cascade Locks, OR 97014
941-400-0050
www.HeartoftheGorgeSailing.com

☐ **Cascade Locks Stop:** Sacagawea Bronze Statue

See this beautiful larger-than-life bronze statue of Sacagawea, (Sah-cog-a-way) as well as Captain Meriwether Lewis' Newfoundland dog, Seaman, located outside the Visitor Center and Locks Waterfront Cafe at 299 SW Portage Rd., Cascade Locks.

To Leave Cascade Locks

Your next and last stop for the day is at the historic Columbia Gorge Hotel in Hood River. To read the directions on how to leave Cascade Locks, see the "Driving Directions" at the end of the description for The Columbia Gorge Hotel on page 55.

☐ **Next *Look*:** Historic Broughton Flume

As you begin to approach Hood River on I-84, you'll see a large freeway sign on the right that reads *Exit 58 - Mitchell Point Overlook.* Do not take this exit, but at this point, while you're driving, look directly ahead to the opposite shore of the Columbia River and you'll spot a gray horizontal ribbon of old timbers and planks crossing a field of rocks just above the river. These boards are the remains of the historic Broughton Flume, a raised wooden flume, or channel of water, which carried rough-cut lumber from a sawmill in Willard, WA to the Broughton Mill at Hood, WA, on the bank of the Columbia River. Long since abandoned, it is slowly decaying at the hands of time. You'll learn more about the Broughton Flume when you pass by it on the northern side of the Columbia River during Day 4 of your road trip.

Photo courtesy of the History Museum of Hood River County.

Tonight's Lodging
Columbia Gorge Hotel - Hood River, Oregon

Historic Columbia Gorge Hotel - 1930s

The first day of your Mt. Hood and Columbia River Gorge road trip ends at the elegant Columbia Gorge Hotel & Spa. Built in 1921 to serve the travelers of the still new Columbia River Highway, the hotel today welcomes guests with 40 romantic guestrooms featuring views of the Columbia River or the hotel's tranquil gardens. Guests will enjoy contemporary furnishings, including King, Queen, or Double beds, and all rooms feature a private bathroom. In addition, select rooms offer antique canopy beds and a fireplace.

And for those who wish to unwind after a day of traveling, The Spa at The Columbia Gorge Hotel offers the perfect menu of treatments to end your day. Enjoy massages, skin or body treatments, natural nail and hair services, and more. The spa is open Thursday through Monday: 10:00 a.m. to 6:00 p.m. - Other appointment times may be available. 541-387-8451 - spa@ColumbiaGorgeHotel.com

The award-winning Columbia Gorge Hotel also offers dining at its Simon's Cliff House Restaurant and Valentino Lounge, with dining on an outdoor terrace during warm summer evenings being an excellent way to finish your day.

Note: Before leaving the hotel, be sure to take the time to wander its landscaped grounds and enjoy Wah-Gwin-Gwin Falls, which falls 207 feet to the Columbia River on the north side of the hotel.

The Columbia Gorge Hotel & Spa
4000 Westcliff Drive
Hood River, OR 97031

Hotel Reservations: 541-386-5566
Spa Reservations: 541-387-8451
Reservations@ColumbiaGorgeHotel.com

- Check-in begins at 4:00 p.m.
- Check-out is at 11:00 a.m.
- Breakfast, lunch and dinner are served at Simon's Cliff House restaurant at the hotel. The hotel's famous Farmer's Breakfast brunch is available on Sundays, beginning at 10:30 a.m. The last seating is at 2:30 p.m.
- Wi-Fi is available in your room and throughout the hotel.
- Up to 2 pets (Dogs only) are welcome at the lodge. Please call 877-411-3436 to reserve a pet friendly room.
- The Columbia Gorge Hotel is a non-smoking property.

Driving Directions: From Cascade Locks...

- Drive east on Wa Na Pa Street through Cascade Locks
- Veer left onto Forest Ln.
- Follow this until it passes over I-84 (If you went to the Easy Trail MTB hike, then you can join here from Industrial Park Way)
- Continue past I-84 and proceed left / east onto Frontage Rd.
- Continue on Frontage Rd. for 0.9 miles and then turn right onto Herman Creek Rd. / Wyeth Rd. Note: This is not the turnoff for the nearby Herman Creek Trailhead, which occurs at .37 miles, though both roads have the same "Herman Creek Rd." name.
- Turn left at 3.6 miles and then turn right onto I-84 Eastbound
- Follow I-84 10.8 miles east to Hood River and take *Exit 62 - W. Hood River - Westcliff Drive.*
- Turn left at the stop and then cross over I-84 and turn left again onto Westcliff Drive. You'll see the Columbia Gorge Hotel on your right. (Note: Do not take the turn for the Columbia Cliff Villas)

Lodging Option: The Hood River Hotel

Note: The Columbia Gorge Hotel is only a few miles west of Hood River. As a result, if there are no rooms available at The Columbia Gorge Hotel for this evening, then go ahead and book two nights at tomorrow night's hotel, the Hood River Hotel, which is located in "old town" Hood River. (See Page 70) Conversely, if there are no rooms available at the Hood River Hotel tomorrow night, then make reservations for two nights at the Columbia Gorge Hotel, beginning tonight.

Hood River Hotel
102 SW Oak Street
Hood River, OR 97031
541-386-1900

Day Two

Explore Hood River

Mitchell Point Tunnel - Historic Columbia River Highway

DAY 2
EXPLORE HOOD RIVER

Day 2 - Date: / /

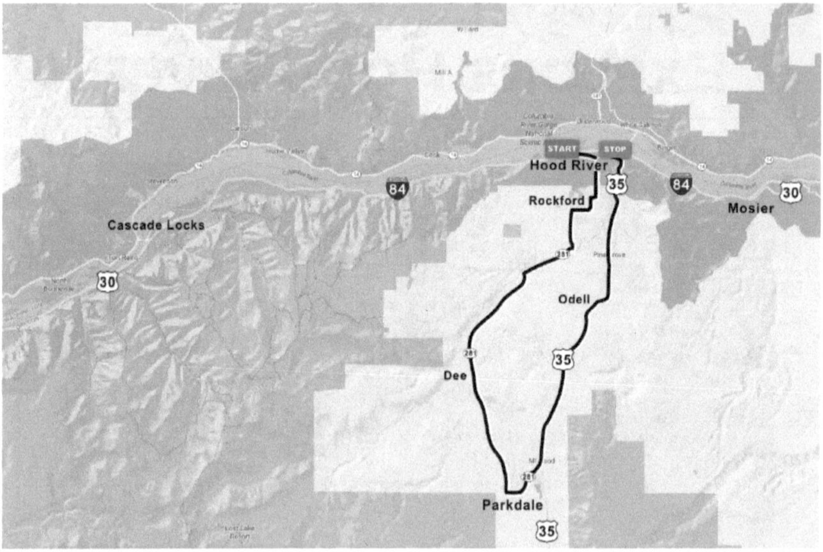

Summary: Where You're Going Today

- Hood River, OR
- The Hood River Fruit Loop

Today you explore the busy town of Hood River, where you'll see an amazing collection of antique planes and automobiles, take to the skies in a historic biplane, walk and shop in "old town" Hood River, enjoy some hand-dipped huckleberry ice cream, travel the famous Hood River Fruit Loop, step into history at a museum or two, watch some world-class sailboarding up close, and taste your new favorite wine for the very first time, all before finishing your day at the historic Hood River Hotel.

Tonight's Lodging:

- The Hood River Hotel

Today's Mileage: 45 Miles

Reservations Needed for This Segment:

- The Hood River Hotel - 541-386-1900
- Biplane Flight - TacAero - 844-359-2827

Before You Leave:

Be mindful of your gas level. There are numerous gas stations in Hood River, including at the south end of the bridge over the Columbia River and south of the "old town" area.

Start

Begin your day by driving to Hood River, where you'll drop right into the "old town" area. You'll explore some destinations here and on the northern end of town, close to the Columbia River, before beginning to make your way south through the Hood River Valley towards Mt. Hood, where you'll begin covering a bit more ground on the Hood River Fruit Loop. Later in the day, you'll return back to the heart of "old town" for your evening's stay at The Hood River Hotel.

Note: You may choose to have breakfast at the Columbia Gorge Hotel & Spa, or if you wish to get started on your travels, you may choose to eat at your first stop of the day, the Egg River Café. Note that this "eggceptional" cafe is very popular with locals, so you may have a wait. Maybe. If it is busy, then you'll want to try Bette's Place just down the road. See both listings on the next page. Note that there is parking for the Egg River Café in the small parking lot across the street, and the peak you see in the distance here is 12,280' Mt. Adams.

Hood River

Home to a busy downtown area filled with recreation-minded folks, the town of Hood River is a launching point for countless outdoor adventures on the eastern end of the Columbia River Gorge National Scenic Area.

☐ **Hood River Stop:** Egg River Café

Whether you're stopping for breakfast or lunch, you'll enjoy the Egg River Café, just as all the locals do. A long menu offers your favorite breakfast items, all made with fresh local ingredients. Enjoy large portions of home-made pancakes and waffles, Egg River skillets, mixed scrambles, breakfast burritos, and even pancake, French toast or waffle sandwiches!

Egg River Café
1313 Oak Street
Hood River, OR 97031
541-386-1127

- Open: Daily - 6:00 a.m. to 2:00 p.m.

Driving Directions: From the Columbia Gorge Hotel, return east on Westcliff Drive a short distance to Cascade Avenue / Hwy 30. Turn right / south onto Cascade Avenue and follow this over I-84. Stay on this road for 1.5 miles from the hotel until you find the Egg River Café on your right, at the light.

Bette's Place

If the wait is too long at the Egg River Café, then head down the road a little ways to the "Friendliest Restaurant in Town", Bette's Place. Here you'll find a full menu of breakfast fare, as well as grandma's warm cinnamon rolls.

Bette's Place
416 Oak Street
Hood River, OR 97031
541-386-1880

- Open: Daily - 5:30 a.m. to 3:00 p.m.

Driving Directions: Bette's Place is on the corner on your left, 1 mile further east from the Egg River Café, on Oak Street.

☐ **Hood River Stop:** Mike's Ice Cream

As you head east down Oak Street towards "old town" Hood River, you'll pass Mike's Ice Cream on your left. It's a bit early for ice cream this morning, so Mike's isn't hopping right now, but later this afternoon and evening, especially if it is warm out, Mike's Ice Cream will be busy! Keep this location in mind if you're in the mood for some delicious hand-scooped ice cream toward the tail end of today. *Note that Mike's accepts only cash or checks.*

Mike's Ice Cream
504 Oak Street
Hood River, OR 97031
541-386-6260

- Open: Daily - April 1 to October 31 - Summer: 11:00 a.m. to 11:00 p.m. - Spring and Fall: Noon-ish to 8:00 p.m....maybe 9:00 p.m. if the day calls for it.

Driving Directions: Mike's Ice Cream is on your left, just shy of 1 mile east from the Egg River Café, on Oak Street.

☐ **Hood River Stop:** Explore Hood River Shops

Oak Street in old town Hood River is home to a collection of interesting shops, stores, boutiques and more. Take some time this morning to walk the street and pop into various shops to see what you just can't live without. Along the way, you'll find bookstores, boutiques, gift shops, a surf shop, bicycle shops, sports shops, a hobby shop, a shop for your dog, and a kids shop named G Willikers Toy Shoppe. That's a lot of shops!

Driving Directions: You'll find most (but not all) of the shops in Hood River on Oak Street, east of Mike's Ice Cream. Park anywhere on Oak Street or a side street and walk.

☐ **Hood River Stop:** Western Antique Aeroplane & Automobile Museum (WAAAM)

Stroll among an *amazing* collection of over 130 flight-ready antique aeroplanes, along with over 180 intricately restored automobiles from the 1910s through 1960s, all under two large hangars spanning over 3.5 acres. In addition, visitors will find antique tractors, motorcycles, military vehicles, toys and more.

Western Antique Aeroplane & Automobile Museum
1600 Air Museum Rd.
Hood River, OR 97031
541-308-1600

- Open Daily 9:00 a.m. - 5:00 p.m. - Closed Thanksgiving Day, Christmas Day and New Years Day

Driving Directions: From the corner of Oak Street and North 2nd Street, proceed west on Oak Street for 0.6 miles to 13th Street. Turn left onto 13th Street and proceed 0.7 miles to where 13th Street becomes 12th Street. Continue south another 2.2 miles as 12th Street becomes Tucker Road, making a couple of 90 degree turns before reaching Air Museum Road and the Western Antique Aeroplane & Automobile Museum.

Hood River Stop: Fly in a Historic Biplane

"Discover Oregon's scenic *flyways* by day, while staying in historic hotels by night."

There is a lot to discover during your Mt. Hood road trip, but the highlight would have to be taking to the skies and seeing the area's beauty in a bright red 1942 Waco UPF-7 biplane!

Enjoy your up-front seat for two in the open cockpit as you fly around Hood River, above the Columbia River Gorge, and even take a flight around Mt. Hood during a longer excursion. It's an amazing Oregon adventure you'll never forget! Have a group of two or three? Then make the same flight in TacAero's enclosed Cessna 172 and ride all together.

Pricing per flight - (Not per person) - Up to 2 passengers:

20 Minutes: $240 - Columbia River & Hood River
45 Minutes: $450 - Hood River valley & Mt. Hood views

Note that reservations are required, and can be made by calling 844-359-2827. Please make your reservations at least one week in advance, and note that flights may be cancelled due to the weather. At least 24 hours advance notice is requested for any flight cancellations. The combined weight of two passengers cannot exceed 310 pounds.

TacAero
3608 Airport Road
Hood River, OR 97031
844-359-2827

- Open: Year-round - Monday through Saturday - Summer: 8:00 a.m. to 6:00 p.m. - Winter: 8:00 a.m. to 4:00 p.m.

Driving Directions: From WAAAM, return to Tucker Road and turn left / west. Follow this as it turns south and in ½ mile, turn left / east onto Airport Road. You'll find TacAero at the end of the road.

☐ **Hood River Stop:** Hood River Fruit Loop & Winery Tour

The Hood River Valley is known around the world for its fruit, as well as its award-winning wines. All throughout the valley you'll find orchard after orchard of apple, pear, peach, and cherry trees, as well as rows of grape vines, growing their delicious fruit in the perfect Oregon summertime weather. Of course, you can't have fruit without pollination, and during the month of April, all of the orchards come to life in an explosion of pink and white blossoms, which is celebrated in a number of Hood River Blossom Festival events throughout the month. If you are traveling during April, check online beginning in March at http://hoodriver.org/celebrate-blossom-time-in-hood-river/ to see this year's schedule, dates, and events.

And when summer comes to a close, then it's time for the fall harvest, and that calls for a celebration, as well. In addition to an abundance of fresh picked fruit and fine wines being offered all along the Fruit Loop, visitors will find the annual

Hood River Valley Harvest Fest occurring for three days in mid-October down at the Event Site by the Columbia River. Visit www.HoodRiver.org/Harvest-Fest/ to learn about this year's dates, hours, and schedule of events.

Traversing all of these attractions is the 35-mile Fruit Loop. This self-guided tour visits nearly 30 different farms, wineries and vineyards offering fresh fruit, jams, jellies, syrups, fruit smoothies, ciders, baked goods, flowers, local artisan gifts, and of course, award-winning wines. Pick up a Fruit Loop map while visiting local shops in Hood River, or download one online and plan on spending a couple of hours making the tour. *Mt. Hood and Barn Photo © Peter Marbach*

☐ **Hood River Stop:** Hood River Valley Lavender Farms

Colorful and aromatic, beautiful Lavender thrives in the Oregon climate. Travelers will often find acres of its blossoms neatly aligned in rows and beckoning artists, photographers, painters and of course honey bees and bumble bees that are attracted to its pleasing scent and bright profusion of purple color. Lavender blooms for much of the summer in Oregon, and peaks during the month of July.

Here are two Lavender Farms located in Hood River Valley, both of which are on the Hood River Fruit Loop.

Hood River Lavender Farm - Fruit Loop Stop #11

With over 70 varieties of organic Lavender, the Hood River Lavender Farm offers acres of plants blooming in the shadow of Mt. Hood. In addition to being able to cut your own bouquets, visitors will find a large variety of Lavender related items for sale, including soap, tea, perfume, oils, culinary products, aromatherapy items, dried Lavender flowers and more.

Hood River Lavender Farms
3801 Straight Hill Road
Hood River, OR 97031 (541-354-9917)

- Open:

  May through September - Wednesday through Saturday - 10:00 a.m. to 5:00 p.m., Sunday 11:00 a.m. to 5:00 p.m.

  October - Friday and Saturday - 10:00 a.m. to 5:00 p.m., Sunday 11:00 a.m. to 5:00 p.m.

Hope Ranch Lavender - Fruit Loop Stop #8

Visit Hope Ranch Lavender and cut a bouquet for yourself or loved ones, shop their farm stand for hand-crafted Lavender products and art pieces made right there on the farm, or just bring a picnic lunch and enjoy the beautiful view of Mt. Hood.

Hope Ranch Lavender
2585 Fir Mountain Road
Hood River, OR 97031 (541-399-4634)

- Open: June until September

☐ **Hood River Stop:** The Hutson Museum

Located in a small building reflecting the historic 1900 Ries-Thompson home next door, the Hutson Museum offers an interesting mix of items showcasing the cultural and natural history of the area, including Native American artifacts, an impressive display of rocks and minerals, military items from WWI and WWII, and more. Admission: $1.00

The Hutson Museum
4967 Baseline Drive
Mt. Hood, OR 97041

- Open: 11:30 a.m. to 3:00 p.m. - Thursday through Sunday - April through October.

Driving Directions: While not listed on the tour map, the Hutson Museum can be found between Stops #14 and #15 on the Hood River Fruit Loop, on Baseline Drive.

☐ **Hood River Stop:** Apple Valley Country Store - Fruit Loop Stop #22

Huckleberries are kind of a big deal on Mt. Hood, and appearing as Stop #22 on The Fruit Loop is the quaint Apple Valley Country Store & Bakery, which features hand-scooped huckleberry ice cream and milkshakes, as well as a wide selection of locally made items, including pies, jams, and jellies, all with fresh ingredients from local farmers. Inside, you'll find nice folks, and outside you'll find seating amongst the dahlias next to the Hood River. It's also a great place to stop at if you're cycling in the area.

Apple Valley Country Store
2363 Tucker Road
Hood River, OR 97031
541-386-1971

Driving Directions: The Apple Valley Country Store is Stop #22 on the Hood River Fruit Loop.

☐ **Hood River Stop:** Watch World-Class Kiteboarders and Sailboarders

Hood River is one of the two best places in the world for kiteboarding and sailboarding, with the other being Hawaii. Visit the "Event Site" to park, get out and watch all of the action up close.

Driving Directions: From the Fruit Loop, return to the corner of Oak Street and North 2nd Street in Hood River. From here, proceed north on North 2nd Street as it crosses over I-84 and works its way down to the Event Site at the 0.4 mile mark.

☐ **Hood River Stop:** Solstice Wood Fire Cafe & Bar

If it's time for lunch or dinner, then you'll want to check out one of our favorite places, Solstice Wood Fire Cafe & Bar. Down by the Event Center and always busy, it offers pizzas and Italian fare showcasing local and Pacific Northwest ingredients, all in a fun and friendly environment with heated outdoor seating, wood burning fireplaces, and river views.

Solstice Wood Fire Cafe & Bar
501 Portway Ave.
Hood River, OR 97301
541-436-0800

Driving Directions: From the Event Center, drive west on Portway Avenue for a few blocks and find Solstice on your left.

☐ **Hood River Stop:** History Museum of Hood River County

The Columbia River has been an important element in the history of this region for ages. With a course carved by ancient and powerful geologic forces, it has provided sustenance to Native Americans for countless generations, while its near sea-level path through the Cascade Mountain Range has attracted early explorers, pioneers, farmers, trappers, and industrialists. Visit the History Museum of Hood River County to learn of the fascinating natural, cultural, agricultural, and recreational history of this region and the Columbia River Gorge.

The History Museum of Hood River County
300 E Port Marina Dr.
Hood River, OR 97031
541-386-6772

- Open: Monday through Saturday - 11:00 a.m. to 4:00 p.m. - Closed during the month of January.

Driving Directions: From the Event Site, return to I-84 on North 2nd Street and take the onramp to I-84 Eastbound. Stay in the right lane and take the first exit, *Exit 64 - White Salmon - Government Camp.* Proceed to the end of the exit and turn left. (Onto Button Bridge Rd.) Before reaching the toll bridge over the Columbia River, turn left at the second light onto East Marina Way / East Port Marina Dr. and follow this west for 0.3 miles to the museum, on your left.

TONIGHT'S LODGING
THE HOOD RIVER HOTEL - HOOD RIVER, OR

Built in 1911, the historic Hood River Hotel's rooms and suites welcome guests with luxurious accommodations, including European style linens, fluffy pillows and down duvets, eco-friendly spa-quality bath products, flat screen TVs, Wi-Fi, and views of the city or nearby Columbia River.

Being in the heart of "old town" Hood River, you'll be close to all kinds of cafes, coffee shops, wineries, and brew pubs. In addition, you can dine at a nearby eatery, or enjoy a meal at Broder Ost, the hotel's European inspired restaurant, before relaxing and enjoying a glass of wine in front of the wood burning fireplace in the lobby. *Hood River Hotel Photo © Ian Poellet*

- Check in: 4:00 p.m.
- Check out: 11:00 a.m.
- Pets are welcome - Inquire when making reservations

Hood River Hotel
102 SW Oak Street
Hood River, OR 97031
541-386-1900

Driving Directions: From the History Museum, return to Burton Bridge Road and turn right / south. Follow this under I-84 and then up and west, as it makes a sweeping turn south to a 4-way stop. Turn right here onto East State Street and follow this 0.4 miles to Front Street. Turn right onto Front Street and follow this around to the corner of 1st Street and Oak Street, where you'll find the Hood River Hotel on the corner on the right.

Lodging Option #1: Old Parkdale Inn B & B

Choose to stay at the Old Parkdale Inn Bed & Breakfast and you'll be treated to the warm hospitality of the owners, Steve and Mary Pellegrini. Located at the halfway point of the Mt. Hood Scenic Byway, and "this close" to Mt. Hood itself, this 1910 Craftsman home welcomes guests with three quaint rooms, each offering queen beds, luxurious beddings, flat screen TVs, private baths, free Wi-Fi and more. Better yet, right outside your door is the Hood River Fruit Loop, which you can spend all day exploring after enjoying a delicious breakfast featuring fresh fruits from the Hood River Valley. Note that the inn features an Electric Vehicle Charging Station.

Old Parkdale Inn Bed & Breakfast
4932 Baseline Drive
Parkdale, OR 97041
541-352-5551

Note: The Old Parkdale Inn B & B is located only a couple of blocks east of The Hutson Museum. (Page 66)

Lodging Option #2: Oak Street Hotel

The historic Oak Street Hotel reaches back to 1909, when it was built as a home in the early days of Hood River, before the completion of the Columbia River Highway. Beautifully restored, this award-winning hotel welcomes guests with small rooms filled with character, as well as refined amenities. Hand-forged iron queen beds, hand-crafted furniture, specially formulated bath products and more all await guests after a day of exploration. Note that while all rooms have en-suite bathrooms, some rooms have a bath separated only by a plush drapery curtain, so be sure to inquire if you wish to have more privacy during your stay.

Breakfast is served buffet style and consists of local farm fresh ingredients, freshly roasted local coffee, and tea service. A Brown Bag Breakfast to-go is also available with advance notice.

Oak Street Hotel
610 Oak Street
Hood River, OR 97031
541-386-3845

NOTES

DAY THREE

HOOD RIVER TO DUFUR

Rowena Loops - Historic Columbia River Highway

DAY 3
HOOD RIVER TO DUFUR

Day 3 - Date: / /

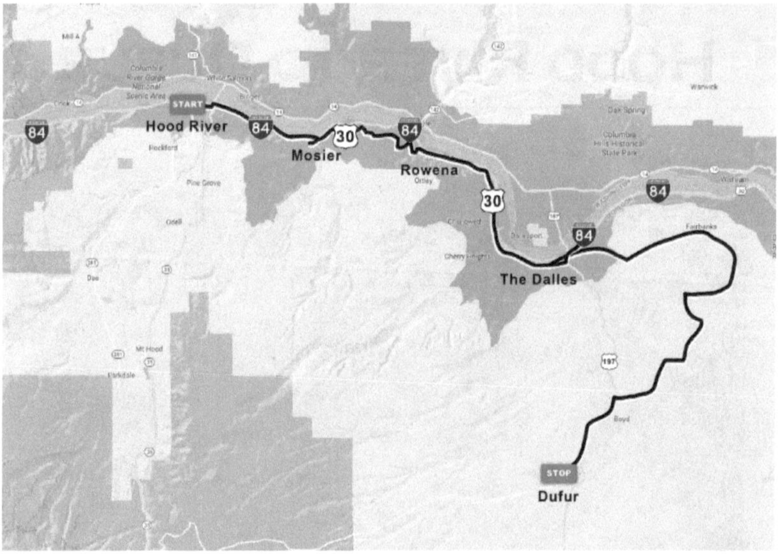

Summary: Where You're Going Today

- Mosier, OR
- Rowena Crest
- The Dalles, OR
- Dufur, OR

Today you'll travel a picturesque and scenic stretch of the Columbia River Highway to the small town of Mosier and the historic Mosier Tunnels. From here, you'll motor to the captivating views of Rowena Crest before continuing on to The Dalles, where you'll explore a number of interesting sites and attractions. Your day winds up with a bit of history, as you make your way to the old Petersburg School and then your final destination for the day, (and one of our favorites) the 1907 Balch Hotel.

Tonight's Lodging:

- The Balch Hotel

Today's Mileage: 47 Miles

Reservations Needed for This Segment:

- The Balch Hotel - 541-467-2277
- Tour of The Dalles Dam - Call 1 day in advance - 541-296-9778
- Nichols Art Glass - Call to see if they are open today - 541-296-2143

Before You Leave:

If you need to get gas, you can get it down by the Hood River Bridge. Take the first exit after you get onto I-84 this morning, pass north / left under I-84, and you'll see two gas stations to the right.

Start

You'll get onto I-84 Eastbound first thing this morning before getting off the freeway 5.7 miles later at the small town of Mosier, OR. From here, you'll travel the historic Columbia River Highway into The Dalles.

To get to I-84 Eastbound from the Hood River Hotel, drive west on Oak Street for one block to the corner of Oak Street and North 2nd Street. Turn right / north onto North 2nd Street and proceed to the onramp for I-84 Eastbound.

MOSIER

☐ **First Stop:** Mosier, OR - Mosier Twin Tunnels Hike

Closed to motorized traffic, the paved Historic Columbia River Highway State Trail takes visitors along the old Columbia River Highway to the Mosier Twin Tunnels, two impressive tunnels blasted into the basalt cliffside nearly 100 years ago. Inspired by the design of the Axenstrasse on Lake Lucerne, Switzerland, the tunnels were built with large viewing portals and observation walkways offering travelers a unique view of the gorge. Of note is the inscription carved into the rock on the north side wall at the east end of the tunnels. It reads...

Snowbound
November 19 to 27, 1921
Chas J. Sadilek
E. B. Marvin

Note that there is an abundance of wildflowers growing in this area during the months of April and May, with the peak occurring in mid- to late-April.

Driving Directions: From the Hood River Hotel, proceed east on I-84 and take Exit 69 for Mosier, OR and Hwy 30. Turn right onto Hwy 30 / Historic Columbia River Highway Scenic Byway.

At 0.15 miles, turn left / north onto Rock Creek Rd. and follow this 0.6 miles west to the large paved parking area on the left. Park, pay the parking fee, and then hike back down the road a short distance to the trailhead. Hike from here on the paved road 0.8 miles to the old Mosier Tunnels and viewpoint. The road is closed to cars, but open to cyclists and pedestrians, so be sure to stay to the right as you walk.

Note: While driving from Hood River to Mosier on I-84, you can spot the west entrance to the Mosier Tunnels, as well as some of the viewing windows, up on the cliffside immediately after passing the freeway sign that reads *Exit 69 - Mosier 1 Mile.*

The Story of Chas J. Sadilek & E.B. Marvin

On November 19, 1921, Chas Sadilek was returning home to Portland from a goose hunting trip when he was caught in a powerful November snowstorm, one which stranded nine passenger trains throughout the Gorge and dropped 54 inches of snow on The Dalles, a town which typically receives only 14 inches of snow per year. Though he was still quite close to the small town of Mosier, the snow had become so deep that driving had become impossible, so he, along with 10 other cars filled with travelers, sought shelter in the Mosier tunnels, a series of long tunnels carved into the cliffside basalt just west of Mosier. Fortunately for Mr. Sadilek, his Hudson was filled with camping supplies and no doubt a few fat geese. He was more than prepared to ride out the storm. Receiving word that travelers were stranded in the tunnels, the state highway department cleared a path to their entrance and escorted those who wanted to leave two miles down to Mosier, where they could rent motel rooms and find a warm meal. Mr. Sadilek, along with another man, Mr. Marvin, chose to stay in the tunnels so that they would not have to leave their cars.

Sometime during their 8 day adventure, the two men carved into a smooth stone face at the east end of the Mosier tunnels an inscription that reads, "*Snowbound, Nov 19 to 27 - 1921, Chas J. Sadilek, E. B. Marvin*".

☐ **Next Stop:** Mosier Plateau Trail

A relatively short hike along Mosier Creek to the Mosier Plateau rewards hikers with a grand view, as well as an abundance of wildflowers in April and May. Find the trail heading south at the east end of the old bridge in Mosier. Hike past Mosier Creek Falls, up four sets of stairs and switchbacks, and you're there. 3.5 Miles roundtrip, and approximately 2 miles if you hike to only the first viewpoint.

Driving Directions: From the Mosier Twin Tunnels trailhead, head back east the way you came and continue east on the Historic Columbia River Scenic Byway / Hwy 30 into Mosier. Do not return to I-84 Eastbound. As you pass through town, you'll come to a short narrow bridge. Immediately after the bridge, you'll see the trailhead for the Mosier Plateau Trail on the right. Parking for the trail can be found in the large gravel lot at the west end of the bridge, marked *Mosier Plateau Trail Parking.*

☐ **Next Stop:** Randonnée Coffee Co.

After the Mosier Plateau Hike, you may wish to stop in at the Randonnée Coffee Co. Enjoy a selection of hot coffees featuring freshly roasted beans, an artisan bakery treat, or a hearty sandwich, all on their outdoor patio or inside their renovated rustic shop. Keep in mind that Randonnée Coffee Co. closes at 3:00 p.m. on most days.

Randonnée Coffee Co.
1104 1st Ave.
Mosier, OR 97040

□ **Next Stop:** Rowena Crest Viewpoint / Tom McCall Nature Preserve

This "must stop" location gives travelers a commanding view of the east end of the Columbia River Gorge, a walk among plateaus covered in colorful spring wildflowers, and a high vantage point over the picturesque Rowena Loops of the old Columbia River Highway.

Note: Two short hikes may be made both above and below the parking area for Rowena Crest. The upper hike begins on the south side of the parking area and continues 1.8 miles to the summit of McCall Point. The lower trail, which begins to the west and opposite the turn into Rowena Crest, passes through wildflower meadows that bloom from late February through June, peaking in April and May. Early to mid-May offers an abundance of the brilliant yellow flowers of the Arrowleaf Balsamroot. Note that picking flowers is not permitted, and be mindful of the poison oak in this area, as well as ticks.

Driving Directions: Continue to follow the Historic Columbia River Highway Scenic Byway / Hwy 30 for 6.6 miles east from Mosier to Rowena Crest.

THE DALLES

Your next set of stops are in The Dalles, a town which showcases the ancient, rich and dramatic history of the eastern end of the Columbia River Gorge, as reflected in its archaeological sites, historical buildings, ornate Victorian and Gothic style homes, and fascinating museums.

☐ **The Dalles Stop:** Columbia Gorge Discovery Center & Museum

At over 48,000 square feet, the Columbia Gorge Discovery Center & Wasco County Historical Museum showcases a vast array of exhibits which explain the many wonders of this area, including the forces that shaped the Columbia River Gorge, the 10,000 year old culture of the gorge's native inhabitants, the journey of Lewis & Clark, and much more.

Columbia Gorge Discovery Center & Museum
5000 Discovery Drive
The Dalles, OR 97058
541-296-8600

- Open Daily: 9:00 a.m. - 5:00 p.m.

Driving Directions: From the Rowena Crest Viewpoint, continue down into the Rowena Loops from Rowena Crest and proceed on the Historic Columbia River Highway Scenic Byway / Highway 30 east towards The Dalles. At 7.0 miles from Rowena Crest, turn left / east onto Discovery Drive, which leads you under I-84 and back north to the Columbia Gorge Discovery Center & Museum.

☐ **The Dalles Stop:** The Dalles Riverfront Trail

Traversing the south bank of the Columbia River for 10 paved miles between The Columbia Gorge Discovery Center & Museum on its west end and (eventually) The Dalles Dam Visitor Center on its east end, The Dalles Riverfront Trail makes for a nice stroll or bike ride along the Columbia River to downtown, Riverfront Park, The Dalles Marina, and elsewhere. Find a map of the trail at The Columbia Gorge Discovery Center trailhead. Note that the first two miles of the trail leading from The Columbia Gorge Discovery Center are perhaps the most scenic.

Walking Directions: You'll find the start of The Dalles Riverfront Trail at the entrance to the parking lot for the Columbia Gorge Discovery Center & Museum.

☐ **The Dalles Stop:** Klindt's Booksellers

The next chapter of your road trip takes you to Klindt's Booksellers, the oldest bookstore in Oregon. Selling books since 1870, and from this bookstore since 1893, its shelves offer an abundance of titles, including an impressive collection of new books every month. You can even find our Oregon Road Trip books here!

Klindt's Booksellers
315 E. 2nd Street
The Dalles, OR 97058
541-296-3355

- Open Monday - Saturday: 8:00 a.m. - 6:00 p.m.
- Sunday: 11:00 a.m. - 4:00 p.m.

Driving Directions: From the Discovery Center, continue east on the Historic Columbia River Highway Scenic Byway / Highway 30 into The Dalles and stay on Hwy 30 as it automatically turns into W 6th St. (Continue straight - Do not turn left onto Webber St.) Continue on W 6th St. as it veers leftward onto W 3rd Place before joining E. 3rd Street. Follow this and then turn left / north onto Federal St. Park in street parking spots just across E. 2nd Street and walk west to Klindt's Booksellers.

☐ **The Dalles Stop:** City of The Dalles Fire Museum

This small self-guided museum offers a unique taste of Oregon history with its two old-fashioned steam-powered fire engines from the 1800s, as well as an interesting collection of antique fire-fighting equipment, artifacts and photos.

City of The Dalles Fire Museum
313 Court Street
The Dalles, OR 97058
541-296-5481 - xt 1119

- Located inside City Hall
- Free Admission
- Closed on Weekends
- Open Monday - Friday 8:00 a.m. - 5:00 p.m.

Walking Directions: From Klindt's, *walk* west on E 2nd Street for 1.5 blocks to Court Street. Turn left / south and walk 1 block to the City Hall building at 313 Court Street. Walk in the front door, through the hallway and down the stairs to the museum in the back.

☐ **The Dalles Stop:** National Neon Sign Museum

Located in the stately 1910 Elks Lodge in The Dalles is the fascinating National Neon Sign Museum. Here, you'll find a growing collection of colorful signs from the past, many of which you may recognize, and all arranged with interpretive displays that walk visitors through the chronological history of store front advertising, beginning with the simple reflective signs of the mid-19th century before progressing to signs lit by the new incandescent light bulb in the late 1800s, with colorful neon then following in 1910.

Be sure to make your way upstairs to walk among a collection of creative storefront facades, including Verne's Television Repair, Peggy's Beauty Shop, Chapman's Ice Cream, Medich's Steaks & Chicken & BBQ diner, and, of course, Frank Neon Sign Co., all attracting customers with their colorful neon signs.

National Neon Sign Museum
200 East 3rd Street
The Dalles, OR 97058

- Open: Thursday through Saturday - 10:00 a.m. to 5:00 p.m.

Walking Directions: From The Dalles Fire Museum, walk to the National Neon Sign Museum, which is just across the street, on the opposite corner.

☐ **The Dalles Stop:** Old St. Peter's Landmark

Standing majestically over the city, the Old St. Peter's Landmark is a former Catholic Church that today serves as a beautiful historical museum. Built in 1897 with an ornate Gothic Revival architectural style, it features tall and colorful stained glass windows, a wooden Madonna carved from the keel of a sailing ship, imported Italian marble, and a towering spire which is the highest found in the Columbia River Gorge.

405 Lincoln Street
The Dalles, OR 97058
541-296-5686

- Free admission

Walking Directions: From the National Neon Sign Museum, walk west on E 3rd Street for three blocks to the church.

☐ **The Dalles Stop:** Fort Dalles Museum and Anderson Homestead

Dating back to 1905, the impressive Fort Dalles Museum is one of Oregon's two oldest history museums. Here you'll wander through a collection of original buildings from the 1856 Fort Dalles military compound, each offering a themed display of rare artifacts and items reflecting the amazing history of the area and its early pioneers. In addition, you'll find a barn filled with over 30 antique horse-drawn wagons and automobiles. Note: Be sure to ask to hear the working Edison Phonograph!

500 West 15th and Garrison
The Dalles, OR 97058
541-296-4547

- Open Monday - Sunday: 10:00 a.m. - 5:00 p.m. - March through November.
- Closed December, January and February.

Driving Directions: Head back to your car and, from Klindt's Booksellers, drive west on E 2nd Street for 2.5 blocks to Union Street. Turn left / south onto Union Street and proceed for 0.6 miles to E 14th Street. Turn right / west here and follow this for 4 blocks to Garrison Street. Turn left here and continue one block to the museum.

☐ **The Dalles Stop:** Rorick House Museum

At over 165 years old, the small Malcolm A. Moody House, home of the Rorick House Museum, is the oldest remaining house in The Dalles.

The Rorick House Museum
300 W 13th St.
The Dalles, OR 97058

- Open only during the summer months

Driving Directions: From the Fort Dalles Museum, drive north on Garrison Street for 2 blocks to W 13th Street. Turn right here and continue two blocks to the Rorick House on your right.

☐ **The Dalles Stop:** Nichols Art Glass

Stop in at Nichols Art Glass, grab a seat, and watch as Andy Nichols and his team practice their craft. As personable as he is skilled at the art of glassblowing, Andy will answer any questions you may have as he works to create the pieces which are displayed in galleries, private collections, and exhibits around the world. His specialty is the creation of stunning salmon and trout, each of which takes 1.5 to 2 hours to bring to life.

Visitors to Nichols Art Glass are more than welcome, but call first to see if the shop is open and Andy or his staff will be blowing glass when you're in town. In a nutshell, Nichols Art Glass is open when it's open, so there are no set hours.

Nichols Art Glass
912 W 6th Street
The Dalles, OR 97058
541-296-2143

By the way, **Mama Jane's Pancake House** across the parking lot is very good.

Driving Directions: From the Rorick House, return west on W 13th Street for 3 blocks to Trevitt Street. Turn right / north onto Trevitt Street and follow this for 0.4 miles to W 6th Street. Turn left / west onto W 6th Street and follow this 0.2 miles to Nichols Art Glass and Mama Jane's Pancake House on your left.

☐ **The Dalles Stop:** The Dalles Dam Visitor Center

The massive Dalles Dam is a "powerhouse" for the region's economy. Finished in 1957, it has generated nearly 10 billion kilowatt hours of electricity, while facilitating the passage of 10 million tons of river cargo into and out of the Pacific Northwest's Inland Empire. Stop in at The Dalles Dam Visitor Center to view interpretive displays that explain the impact of the dam from numerous perspectives, including those of the world of agriculture, power, recreation, travel, fishing, and more. Then step outside to explore the over one mile of walking trails leading to the foundations of the old Seufert Cannery and its fish wheel, as well as the historic Seufert Rose Garden, which is home to more than 90 varieties of antique roses planted by Mrs. Seufert over 100 years ago. There is no admission charge for visiting the Visitor Center.

Free tours of the dam are also offered during the summer months, and these occur at 10:00 a.m. and 2:00 p.m. beginning in early May, though times can vary depending upon the availability of personnel. *Call the Visitor Center at least one day in advance to pre-register for the tours, as space is limited.*

The Dalles Dam Visitor Center
3545 Bret Clodfelter Way
The Dalles, OR 97058
541-296-9778

- Open: 9:00 a.m. to 5:00 p.m. - Weekends from May 1 through Memorial Day, and then every day through Labor Day. Open Friday through Sundays from Labor Day until the end of September.

Driving Directions: From Nichols Art Glass, drive west on W 6th Street for 0.6 miles to the entrance to I-84 Eastbound on your right. Merge onto I-84 Eastbound and continue 3.2 miles to *Exit 87 - Dufur - Bend.* Take this exit and turn left / north onto Hwy 197 at the stop. Shortly after crossing I-84 turn right / east onto Bret Clodfelter Way and then continue for 0.8 miles to The Dalles Dam Visitor Center.

☐ **The Dalles Stop:** Eagles at Westrick Park

Located north of The Dalles Dam Visitor Center, across the waterway, is Westrick Park, and every year Bald Eagles return here between mid-/late-December to mid-February to roost in the trees and feed on shad in the river below. Ten years ago, one might have hoped to see 10 eagles roosting in these trees, but today you can spot as many as 60 during the peak period in mid-January!

To see the eagles, walk north of The Dalles Dam Visitor Center, across the parking lot, to the water's edge and look in the trees across the water, in front of the large concrete wall of the dam. Note that if you didn't bring your own binoculars, you will find free stationary binoculars for viewing the eagles mounted atop posts at the Visitor Center.

Photo courtesy of Amber Tilton - US Army Corps of Engineers.

☐ **The Dalles Stop:** Big Jim's Drive-In

If you're getting hungry, you'll find a number of good places in The Dalles at which to eat. One place we really enjoy, especially after a day of cycling southeast of The Dalles, is Big Jim's Drive-In. It's a family style restaurant with nice folks offering sandwiches, soups, salads, hot dogs, and an amazing selection hamburger choices on the menu, all made with fresh ingredients. In addition, you can choose from 16 flavors of Oregon's Umpqua ice cream, as well as milk shakes, sundaes, banana splits, fresh fruit smoothies and more.

Big Jim's Drive-In
2938 E. 2nd Street
The Dalles, OR 97058

- Open: Daily 10:00 a.m. to 10:00 p.m. - Open to 9:00 p.m. in the winter.

As a great alternative, we're also fans of dining at **Cousins' Restaurant**, found at 2114 W 6th Street. 541-298-2771

☐ **Next Stop:** Historic Petersburg School House

A well-preserved historic one room school house that served students in The Dalles area. Note that it is not open to the public.

Historic Petersburg School
15 Mile Road
The Dalles, OR 97014

Driving Directions: From The Dalles Dam Visitor Center, return west on Bret Clodfelter Way for 0.8 miles to Highway 197. Turn left / south here and continue over I-84 to the stop at 0.4 miles. Turn right / west here and then continue 0.2 miles and take the right hand turn just past Big Jim's Drive-In that leads you to SE Frontage Road / State Road. Turn right / east onto SE Frontage Road / State Road and follow this as it turns into Fifteen Mile Road. At 3.2 miles, turn left / northeast onto what is still Fifteen Mile Road. (It's going to seem like Fifteen Mile Road continues straight, but that's now 8 Mile Road.) Drive 0.3 miles and find the school on the left.

Note: The Historic Petersburg School House is a popular starting point for many outstanding cycling routes in this area, all of which head south and east from the school. For an excellent book of cycling routes in Oregon, we highly recommend *75 Classic Rides Oregon: The Best Road Biking Routes* by Jim Moore.

A Whimsical Detour

Want to see a rafter (flock) of wild turkeys? Perhaps anywhere from 20 to 100 of them? Then leave the Petersburg School and return west on 15 Mile Road for 0.3 miles. Turn left / south onto 8 Mile road and immediately begin looking for wild turkeys in the field to your right, usually close to the tree line. If you don't see them here, continue driving a little further south on 8 Mile road, all the while looking for turkeys. You are most likely to see them within the first two miles after your turn. If you are unsuccessful, you may continue driving south on 8 Mile road, where you may spot a different rafter of wild turkeys on either side of the road anytime prior to reaching the five mile mark. Once finished, return to the Petersburg School and continue your road trip.

☐ **Next Stop:** Pathfinders Memorial

High on a road bank, clearly out of place among the wheat fields of the area, stands like a sentinel a single column of basalt. Affixed to its side is a bronze plaque which reads... *Here lie many pathfinders to the Oregon country - Erected by The Wasco County Pioneer Association 1935.* This memorial is dedicated to those Oregon Trail pioneers who lost their lives and were buried in a burial ground adjacent to a nearby campsite used by early pioneers on their way to Fort Dalles in The Dalles.

Driving Directions: From the Historic Petersburg School House, continue east on Fifteen Mile Road for 6.7 miles. You'll spot the lone basalt column up on the bank to the left, just to the side of the road.

TONIGHT'S LODGING THE BALCH HOTEL - DUFUR, OR

The historic 1907 Balch Hotel is a highlight of the trip. Josiah and Claire welcome you with homemade cookies, a refreshing drink, and a slower, genuinely friendly pace before directing you to your well-appointed period-specific room.

In addition to being your third night's stay, the award-winning Balch Hotel is also a fun weekend destination, with a lot of events occurring here throughout the year. Be sure to sign up for their email newsletter to stay in the know.

If your travel timing works out, we highly recommend you dine at the Balch Hotel this evening. Find a table under the string lights on the patio and enjoy the cool evening as you watch the sun set behind Mt. Hood.

Historic Balch Hotel
40 South Heimrich St.
Dufur, OR 97021
541-467-2277
www.BalchHotel.com

- Check in between 3:00 p.m. and 9:00 p.m.
- Dinner and a "delicious house made breakfast" are available - Dining reservations are required.
- To-Go breakfasts are also available with advance notice
- Ask for a room with a Mt. Hood view.
- Stock up for the next day's journey at the Dufur Market in downtown Dufur.
- The Balch Hotel does not accommodate pets.

Note: If it's warm out, then be sure to explore the landscaped grounds, complete with outdoor seating, soft shaded grass, a small pond and a patio.

If you visit the Dufur Market, be sure to walk across the street and look in the windows to see a unique Oregon sight!

Driving directions to the Balch Hotel from the Pathfinders Memorial:

Driving Directions: From the Pathfinders Memorial, continue on Fifteen Mile Road for 3.9 miles to Kelly Cutoff Road. Turn right / west onto Kelly Cutoff Road and follow this for 2.5 miles, where you'll then turn left / south onto Emerson Loop Road. From here, proceed 5.5 miles to Ward Road. Turn left / south onto Ward Rd. and follow this 3.4 miles to Hwy 197. Turn left / south onto Hwy 197 and drive 4 miles to Dufur, OR. Take the exit to Dufur and follow the main road into the heart of town. You'll find the Historic Balch Hotel on your left at 40 Heimrich St.

Lodging Option: Victor Trevitt Guest House

Built in 1868 and recently restored with impeccable period-specific detail and antique furnishings, the historic Victor Trevitt Guest House makes for a nice alternative if the Balch Hotel is full.

The house will accommodate up to 4 guests, with 2 bedrooms, 3 beds and 1.5 baths.

Your hosts, Alan and Bev Eagy, live right next door in the historic 1867 Ben Snipes house, to the west.

Note that the Victor Trevitt Guest House is located in The Dalles, 14 miles north of Dufur.

Victor Trevitt Guest House
214 W 4th Street
The Dalles, OR
541-980-3522

Born in 1827, Victor Trevitt moved to The Dalles in 1853 and as a printer, entrepreneur, businessman, state legislator and the first judge to preside at the small Wasco County Courthouse, he played an important role in shaping the growth of this area and developing The Dalles.

Notes

Day Four

Dufur to Timberline Lodge

Cloud Cap Inn - Circa 1896
Photo courtesy of The History Museum of Hood River County

DAY 4
DUFUR, OR TO TIMBERLINE LODGE

Day 4 - Date: / /

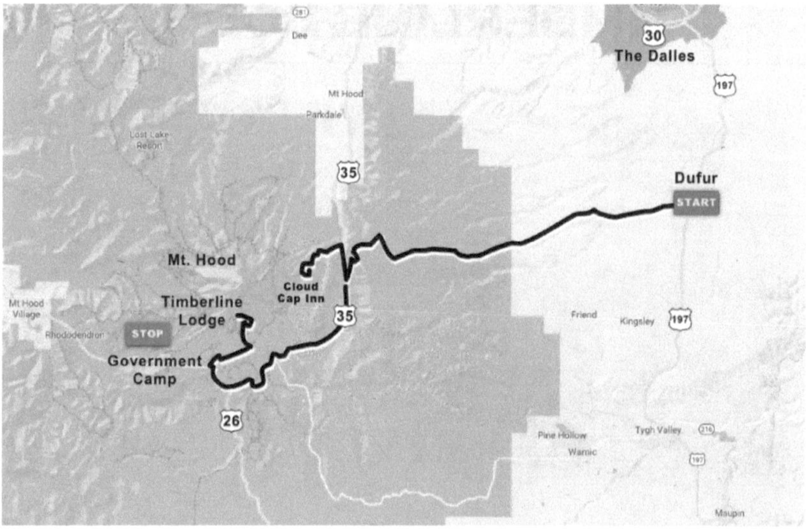

Summary: Where You're Going Today

- Dufur, OR
- Dufur Living History Museum
- Cloud Cap Inn
- Timberline Lodge

Today's activities afford the luxury of a slow start to your day. Take some time to enjoy a leisurely breakfast on the lawn at The Balch Hotel before walking up the street to explore the history of the area in the Dufur Living History Museum. Then begin to make your way toward Mt. Hood, where you have the option of adding some adventure to your day by winding your way up a remote gravel road to the historic Cloud Cap Inn and its stunning up-close views of Mt. Hood.

From here, you're off to the grand Timberline Lodge, where you'll spend the day enjoying the lodge and its surrounding area before calling it a night.

Tonight's Lodging:

- Timberline Lodge

Today's Mileage: 81 Miles

Reservations Needed for This Segment:

- Timberline Lodge - 503-272-3311
- Timberline Lodge Cascade Dining Room Reservations - 503-272-3311
- Hike with the friendly St. Bernards of Timberline Lodge - 800-547-1406

Before You Leave:

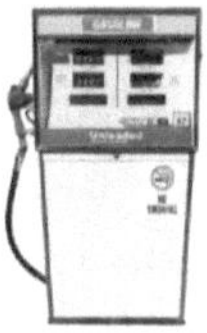

If you're low on gas, then be sure to fill up in Dufur, just north of The Balch Hotel. Note that the price of gas is usually pretty good at the Dufur station. Just park here and someone should come out of the General Store across the street to help you, provided you are there during business hours, which are Monday through Saturday, 8:00 a.m. to 6:00 p.m.

Start

☐ **First Stop:** Dufur Living History Museum

Before leaving Dufur, walk one block north from The Balch Hotel to the Dufur Living History Museum. Here, you can stroll among antique harvesting equipment, hay wagons, buckboards, an old blacksmith shop and more on the grounds outside before stepping into one of the original buildings on the site dating back to the turn of the 20th century. Inside, you'll find many impressive exhibits and displays that depict life in Oregon and the Pacific Northwest during the late 1800s to early 1900s. While you're there, be sure to ask about the story behind the bell atop the old Endersby School. The museum is free, but donations are gladly accepted.

Dufur Living History Museum
40 Main Street
Dufur, OR 97021
541-467-2205

- Open: Wed. through Saturday - 10:00 a.m. to 5:00 p.m.

☐ **Next Stop:** Dufur Market

In one form or another, Dufur Market has been the center of Dufur for over 100 years, since 1905. Inside this old-fashioned store you'll find a busy marketplace offering all kinds of goods, as well as local wines, a restaurant and deli, coffees and smoothies, and tables inside and out at which to enjoy your meal. This is an excellent place to stop if you are cycling, fishing, climbing or hiking out in this part of Oregon. After you visit the Dufur Market, make sure you walk directly across the street to peek into the storefront windows. We won't spoil the surprise.

Dufur Market
121 N Main Street
Dufur, OR 97021
541-467-2455

- Open Daily

MT. HOOD

The early days of exploration on Mt. Hood makes for a fascinating story, as rugged and determined individuals from all walks of life forged a difficult path to the mountain's northern and southern slopes, opening lodges, inns, restaurants, livery stables, transportation services and more to serve those who wished to make their way to the mountain, ski on its slopes, and in many cases climb to its 11,245' summit.

The following two destinations, Cooper Spur Mountain Resort and Cloud Cap Inn, played an important role in Mt. Hood's early history and recreational development.

☐ **Next Stop:** Cooper Spur Mountain Resort

Located at the base of Mt. Hood's northern slopes is the historic Cooper Spur Mountain Resort. This quaint resort offers travelers luxury lodge accommodations, mountain cabins, farm to table dining, and an abundance of year-round activities including downhill and Nordic skiing, all in a rustic mountain lodge setting.

Cooper Spur Mountain Resort
10755 Cooper Spur Road
Mt. Hood, OR 97041
541-352-6692

Driving Directions: From the Balch Hotel, drive south on Heimrich Street 0.2 miles to Dufur Valley Road / NF-44. Turn right / west onto Dufur Valley Road and follow this for 26.7 miles to Highway 35. Turn right / north onto Hwy 35 and follow this for 3.1 miles to Cooper Spur Road. Turn left / west onto Cooper Spur Road / Forest Service Road 3512 from Highway 35 and follow this for 2.3 miles to the resort.

HISTORIC CLOUD CAP INN

High on the eastern flank of Mt. Hood, at an elevation of 6,000', sits Cloud Cap Inn. Built in 1889 with hand-hewn timber and stone from the surrounding area, this historic mountain inn offers visitors dramatic up-close views of Mt. Hood, as well as Oregon's largest glacier, Eliot Glacier. With its centralized location, the inn is used as a base by the Crag Rats, a volunteer group providing rescues on Mt. Hood and the surrounding area, and as such, it is usually not open to the public, but visitors may get lucky when they stop by and find members of the Crag Rats stationed there and offering an opportunity to sit on the patio or peek inside. In addition, there are numerous trails leading from the inn to areas on the east side of Mt. Hood, with the Cooper Spur hike being perhaps the most popular, as it takes hikers up and along the southern lateral moraine of the jumbled Eliot Glacier.

Early entrepreneurs opened the inn with the intention of it becoming a luxury alpine resort. With its quality meals, feather bedding, and sublime mountain views, it commanded a premium price of $5 per night, thus attracting the well-to-do of society. However, reaching the inn proved to be quite difficult, as the rough dirt road cut through the dense forest required four to five hours worth of arduous travel by horse-drawn stages to traverse. As a result, the original owners found few willing to make the journey. In the ensuing years, the building changed ownership a number of times, but began to slowly succumb to neglect in the harsh mountain environment. Violent winter storms, heavy spring snows, summer forest fires, and other battles with the elements began to take their toll on this unique building and it was eventually sold to the Forest Service in 1942. With World War II gripping the nation and all resources going to the war effort, the Forest Service had no time nor budget to maintain the inn, so they considered burning it down. However, in 1954 Oregon's Crag Rats, the oldest search and rescue team in the United States, purchased the inn for $2,000 and they have diligently maintained and cared for it ever since.

While the inn is generally not open to the public, official Forest Service guided tours for the public are offered at 11:00 a.m. and 1:00 p.m. on Sundays during the summer months until Labor Day weekend. For additional information and to sign up for a tour, call the Hood River Ranger District at 541-352-6002. Their office is open Monday through Saturday during the summer, 8:00 a.m. to 4:30 p.m.

Driving Directions: From the Cooper Spur Mountain Resort, connect with Cloud Cap Road, which begins directly across from the resort, and follow this for 11 miles as it turns into a dirt and gravel road making its way up through a burned forest filled with silver snags to a junction for the Tilly Jane Campground and the Cloud Cap Inn. Head right and follow this increasingly rough road for 1 mile as it curves up to the inn. Note that the road is very rough in places but is passable in a passenger car suited for this kind of travel. Visitors will need to display a Northwest Forest Pass on their car dashboard, and a free self-register wilderness permit will need to be filled out at the nearby trailheads if you'd like to do any hiking.

Important: Because of its elevation and unmaintained road, you will want to skip a visit to Cloud Cap Inn if you are traveling between October and mid- to late-June, or if there is *any* snow on the road to the inn. Note that there is no cell service on some sections of the road to Cloud Cap Inn.

For the latest road conditions, call:

- Hood River Ranger District - 541-352-6002
    - Open Monday - Saturday, 8:00 a.m. to 4:30 p.m.

Want to learn more about the history of Cloud Cap Inn, Timberline Lodge, Mt. Hood and the surrounding area? Then we highly recommend two web sites, www.MtHoodHistory.com and www.HistoricHoodRiver.com. Both are filled with rare and unique historical photos, ephemera, stories and personal accounts of days past that you cannot find anywhere else.

☐ **Next Stop:** Hike with Timberline's St. Bernards

As you make your way toward tonight's stay at historic Timberline Lodge, you may want to arrive early enough for a hike with Heidi or Bruno, Timberline Lodge's friendly St. Bernard mascots. You'll check in at the front desk on the 1st floor, and then leave from the lodge on a 45 minute hike (or snowshoe trip if you're arriving during the winter months) on a route that could take you up to Silcox Hut, along the Timberline Trail, through an alpine forest on a leisurely stroll, or wherever your group decides. Bottled water, trail mix, and doggie treats are included.

Cost: $150 per group. Reservations should be made up to a week in advance (minimum 72 hours) by calling 800-547-1406. Available Thursdays through Mondays. Check in at the front desk of the historic lodge at least 15 minutes prior to your departure time. Dress accordingly for the weather, and be sure to use sunscreen during the summer months. Snowshoes are provided for snowshoe hikes, though you'll need to wear your own boots.

Tonight's Lodging - Timberline Lodge

One of Oregon's premier icons, historic Timberline Lodge, set at the 6,000' timberline of Mt. Hood, welcomes visitors with a commanding presence in a lofty alpine setting, with snowy 11,245' Mt. Hood towering above to the north while the summits of the Oregon Cascades stretch far to the south. Guests are welcomed with classic 1930s-era mountain lodge architecture featuring hand-sculpted stonework, a wood beam interior with wrought iron accents, a massive six-sided stone fireplace reaching 92' high, and a complement of 70 cabin-like guest rooms, some of which offer wood-burning fireplaces.

Plan to arrive early enough in the day today to enjoy a number of different activities available to guests, including visiting the museum dedicated to the construction and history of the lodge, which is located on the first floor, riding the ski lift to 7,000' for an up-close look at the mountain and a panoramic view of Oregon, (No skis or snowboards required!) swimming in the heated outdoor pool, exploring one of the many nearby trails, or simply sitting for a spell with a good book by the fireplace to enjoy the historical ambiance of the lodge. If you're a skier or snowboarder and want to enjoy some sunny summertime skiing, then Timberline is the place to do it, as they offer summer skiing every morning until early afternoon late into the season. Learn more about the hours of operation and lift ticket prices on their web site at www.TimberlineLodge.com.

Note that you can also make reservations for two nights, if you'd like more time to enjoy the many activities available at Timberline Lodge.

Overnight guests of the lodge are permitted to park in the upper parking lot, near the entrance to the lodge.

Timberline Lodge
27500 W Leg Road
Timberline Lodge, OR 97028

503-272-3311
www.TimberlineLodge.com

Dining at Timberline Lodge

For dinner this evening, we highly recommend you make reservations for dining in the lodge's Cascade Dining Room, and be sure to ask for a table with a window overlooking the Cascade Mountains to the south when you call.

Driving Directions to Timberline Lodge from Cloud Cap Inn:

From Cloud Cap Inn, return to Hwy 35 and turn right / south. Follow this for 16 miles to where you'll merge onto Highway 26 westbound. Continue on Highway 26 for 2.4 miles to Timberline Highway, which is a two-lane road. Turn right / north here and follow this for 5.5 miles up to Timberline Lodge.

Driving Directions from the Balch Hotel in Dufur, OR to Timberline Lodge - If you are skipping Cloud Cap Inn:

From the Balch Hotel, drive south on Heimrich Street 0.2 miles to Dufur Valley Road / NF-44. Turn right / west onto Dufur Valley Road and follow this for 26.7 miles to Highway 35. Turn left / south onto Highway 35 and follow this for 12.8 miles to where you'll merge onto Highway 26 westbound. Continue on Highway 26 for 2.4 miles to Timberline Highway, which is a two-lane road. Turn right here and follow this for 5.5 miles up to Timberline Lodge. Note: *While paved, do not drive Dufur Valley Road / NF-44 in winter or if there is snow on it.* Check with the front desk at the Balch Hotel as to if the road is currently passable.

If Dufur Valley Road / NF-44 is not passable:

If Dufur Valley Road is not currently passable due to snow, then you'll need to return to The Dalles and take I-84 back west to Hood River. From Hood River, follow Highway 35 south for approximately 38 miles to Highway 26. Merge onto Highway 26 westbound and drive for 2.4 miles to Timberline Highway, which is a two-lane road. Turn right here and follow this for 5.5 miles up to Timberline Lodge.

Shorten Your Road Trip to 2 or 3 days

If you wish to shorten your Mt. Hood road trip to only 2 or 3 days, (perfect for a long weekend!) it's easy to do so. Simply skip Day 2, in which you explore Hood River, and Day 3, where you journey out to The Dalles and The Balch Hotel in Dufur, and instead head south on Highway 35 from Hood River to Timberline Lodge after staying the night in The Columbia Gorge Hotel (Page 53) or the Hood River Hotel. (Page 70) While you "skipped" Day 2 and Day 3, you can still choose all kinds of activities from Day 2 and Day 3 to fit within this schedule.

Driving Directions from the Columbia Gorge Hotel & Spa:

From the hotel, return to I-84 and take the onramp to I-84 Eastbound. Drive east for 2.2 miles and take *Exit 64 - Mt. Hood HWY - Govt. Camp.* At the stop, turn right and follow this for 0.2 miles as the road makes a sweeping leftward curve to a 4-way stop. Proceed straight at the 4-way stop, which will put you onto Hwy 35 southbound. Follow Hwy 35 for 38.2 miles and then merge onto Hwy 26 heading west. Continue on Hwy 26 westbound for 2.4 miles to Timberline Hwy, which is a two-lane road. Turn right / north onto Timberline Hwy and follow this for 5.5 miles as it climbs to Timberline Lodge.

Driving Directions from the Hood River Hotel:

From the hotel, drive east on Oak Street as it winds south for one block to E State Street. Turn left / east onto E State Street and proceed 0.4 miles to a 4-way stop. Turn right / south here onto Highway 35 and follow this southbound for 38.2 miles to where it merges onto Highway 26 westbound. Continue on Highway 26 westbound for 2.4 miles to Timberline Highway, which is a two-lane road. Turn right / north onto Timberline Highway and follow this for 5.5 miles as it climbs to Timberline Lodge.

Day Five

Timberline Lodge to Sandy, OR

A Guest of Timberline Lodge

Day 5
Timberline Lodge to Sandy

Day 5 - Date: / /

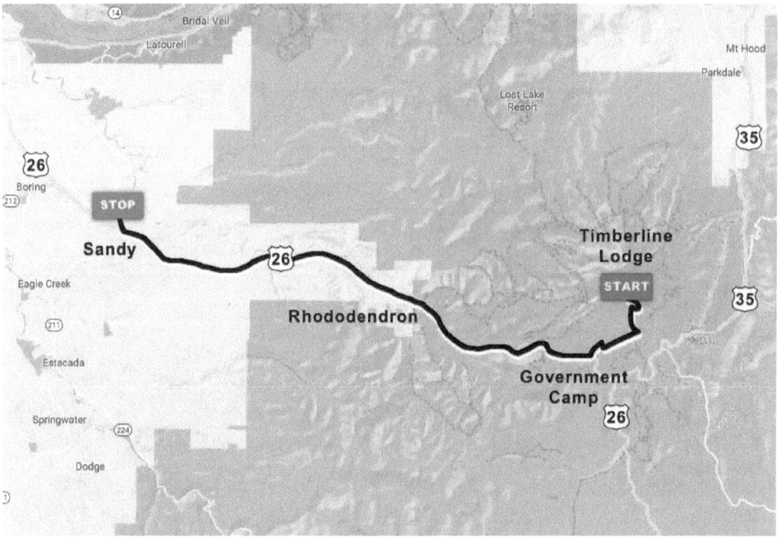

Summary: Where You're Going Today

- Mt. Hood and Timberline Lodge
- Mt. Hood Adventure Park at Skibowl
- Government Camp
- The Barlow Road
- Zig Zag Falls
- Sandy, OR
- Home

The last day of your Mt. Hood road trip takes you along the southwest leg of the Mt. Hood Scenic Byway, where you'll step back through time to explore the fascinating story elements of Mt. Hood's rich history while visiting numerous destinations tied to its past.

Tonight's Lodging:

- Home

Reservations Needed for This Segment:

- Mt. Hood Adventure Park at Skibowl - 503-272-3206

Before You Leave:

If you need to get gas today, you can get it in Government Camp, at the base of the Timberline Highway or West Leg Road. You'll find various shops and restaurants here, as well.

Start

Begin your day by taking a right onto West Leg Road...right into a bit of Timberline Lodge history. Leave the Timberline Lodge parking lot and as you begin to drive downhill, you'll spot a couple of large maintenance buildings on your right, just after you leave the large lower parking area. Shortly after passing these buildings, and approximately 0.5 mile from Timberline Lodge, you'll see a road leading off to the right, the entrance of which is marked with some large concrete blocks. This is West Leg Road, and your first "Stop" for the day.

Note that West Leg Road is open only during the late spring to fall months and is closed in the winter, as it can be covered in more than 12' of snow. If the road is closed, simply continue on the Timberline Highway for 5 miles down to Highway 26 and turn right to access Government Camp in 0.2 mile.

☐ **First Stop:** Historic West Leg Road

Dropping through an alpine forest for a little over 5 miles is the historic West Leg Road. Narrow in spots, roughly paved, and offering scenic views, this was the road used by the Works Progress Administration when they built Timberline Lodge, beginning in 1936. As with the Historic Columbia River Gorge Highway, the West Leg Road was built on a sinuous course through the woods so as to reduce its grade, thus allowing the automobiles of the era, which didn't have the horsepower found in today's vehicles, to traverse its course and make the climb to timberline. Enjoy this drive as it makes its way downhill, passing beneath ski lifts and offering views of the mountain.

Note that this road also makes for an excellent bike ride with little traffic.

☐ **Next Stop:** Mt. Hood Cultural Center & Museum

As the highest point in Oregon, Mt. Hood has a history rich with tales of those who settled this area, lived within the mountain's shadow, opened its slopes to recreation, and dared to explore its many steep faces and lofty frozen summit. Visit the Mt. Hood Cultural Center & Museum to view a large collection of items and exhibits which provide a glimpse into the mountain's history and life on its slopes. You'll also find the "oldest rock on earth" here.

Admission: Free, but donations are gladly accepted.

Mt. Hood Cultural Center & Museum
88900 Government Camp Loop
Government Camp, OR 97028
503-272-3301

- Open: Daily - 9:00 a.m. to 5:00 p.m.

Driving Directions: From Timberline Lodge, drop down West Leg Road to Highway 26 and then drive west for 0.1 mile to Government Camp Loop. Turn right / north onto Government Camp Loop and then proceed west for 0.4 mile to the Mt. Hood Cultural Center & Museum on your left.

☐ **Next Stop:** Mt. Hood Adventure Park at Skibowl

What better way to wrap up the last day of your road trip than with hours of exciting fun and adventure! Make your way to Mt. Hood Adventure Park at Skibowl and choose from over 20 different activities designed for the whole family. Take flight on a zip line, jump from a bungee tower, climb on a rock wall, step up to the plate in a batting cage, ride through the mountain bike park, race along a go-kart track, enjoy the view on the scenic sky chairs, fly down the high-speed alpine slide, and so much more!

Mt. Hood Adventure Park at Skibowl is divided into two sections, Skibowl West and Ski Bowl East, which are separated by approximately 1 mile. Visit their web site at www.skibowl.com/summer to learn about all of the different activities, pricing, ride requirements, etc. *Photo © Mt. Hood Adventure Park at Skibowl*

Skibowl West

- Alpine Slide
- Scenic Sky Chair
- Disc Golf
- Mountain Bike Rentals & Tours
- Mountain Bike Trails and Freeride Park
- Retail Shop & Guest Services
- Beer Stube, Starlight Café & Outback Pizza

Skibowl East

- 32' Rock Wall
- Amaze'n Maze
- Aqua Rollers
- Batting Cages
- Bungee Trampolines
- Disc Golf
- Horseback Rides
- Jacob's Ladder
- Pony Rides
- Summer Tube Hill
- 800' Zip Line
- Freefall Bungee
- Sprint & Indy Race Karts
- Mini Golf
- Tree Top Bridge Tour
- Kiddy Bouldering Wall
- Kiddy Karts
- 70 Meters Bar & Grill, Café, Restrooms and Lockers

Mt. Hood Adventure Park at Skibowl
87000 Highway 26
Government Camp, OR 97028
503-272-3206

- Open:
  - Monday - Thursday: 11:00 a.m. to 6:00 p.m.
  - Friday: 11:00 a.m. to 7:00 p.m.
  - Saturday: 10:00 a.m. to 7:00 p.m.
  - Sunday: 10:00 a.m. to 6:00 p.m.

Driving Directions: The Mt. Hood Adventure Park at Skibowl is located immediately south of Highway 26 at Government Camp and consists of two sections; Skibowl West and Skibowl East, which are separated by approximately one mile. Skibowl East may be reached via E Multorpor Rd. off of Government Camp Loop, the main road through Government Camp, and this provides a convenient bridge for crossing Highway 26. Skibowl West requires travelers to drive across Highway 26, either at the west end of Government Camp Loop or by turning right onto Highway 26 at the west end of Government Camp Loop and traveling west for 0.4 miles to the western entrance to Skibowl West on the left. Note that the *western entrance* may be blocked during the summer months to prevent overflow parking from the adjacent Mirror Lake Trailhead parking area.

☐ **Next Stop:** Hike Part of the Historic Barlow Road

Early pioneers traveling in the mid-1800s by wagon train along the Oregon Trail had two options when crossing the Oregon Cascades; navigate treacherous whitewater on the Columbia River, which could result in capsizing and the loss of all of the possessions needed to begin a new life in Oregon or, if the way wasn't covered in snow or thick with mud, journey around the south flank of Mt. Hood on the Barlow Road. In 1846, Samuel K. Barlow opened the first wagon route over the Cascades, and while there was no danger of capsizing, the way was still extremely difficult. In fact, the passage down Laurel Hill was so steep that wagons had to drag logs behind them so as to keep from careening out of control down the hill and dashing to pieces in the trees.

This next stop allows you to easily hike along a portion of the historic Barlow Road, which passed along the south flanks of Mt. Hood west to the town of Rhododendron and beyond.

Leaving Government Camp on Hwy 26, drive west for approximately ½ mile to where you'll find Glacier View Road / FS Rd 522 on your right, directly across Hwy 26 from the busy parking area for the Mirror Lake trail. Take this road and travel a short distance to where it is blocked by a gate. Park at the trailhead here and walk perhaps 50' into the forest to the north and you'll find the Barlow Road Trail leading west. More than just a trail, this is actually a portion of the Barlow Road. If you choose to follow the trail west, you'll find it splits off to the left in just a short distance and continues to where it is crossed by an old paved road. You may choose to cross the road and continue hiking on the Barlow Road trail as it makes its way through the forest. Note that the paved road you crossed is the old State Hwy 26. This road replaced the Barlow Road beginning in 1923, and it was used to bring visitors to Government Camp and Mt. Hood until the 1950s, when the "new" Hwy 26 was built. Note that this road, along with the West Leg Road, which you descended earlier today, were the routes traveled in 1936 / 1937 by the men and materials used to build Timberline Lodge.

Laurel Hill

As mentioned on the previous page, pioneers making their way west on the Oregon Trail faced a difficult choice when deciding how best to cross the Cascade mountain range...travel north to The Dalles and set out on a raft down the Columbia River with your covered wagon aboard, knowing all the while that the violent drops and fast water of "The Cascades" rapids (near Stevenson) may dash your raft to pieces and send all your worldly possessions to the bottom of the river, or travel south and make your way over the Barlow Road, where the treacherously steep Laurel Hill may dash your covered wagon to pieces across a long rocky drop. Here, the Oregon Trail pioneers would affix a rope to the back of their wagons and then wrap the rope around the trunk of large standing trees, using the trees as a friction brake while slowly lowering the fully loaded wagons, all the while hoping the ropes would not snap under the strain of so much weight. As an option, they would also tie large fallen trees behind their wagons so as to create enough drag to slow and, hopefully, manage their descent down the slope.

You won't be stopping at Laurel Hill today, since the trailhead is difficult to reach while driving in a westward direction down the mountain due to the placement of highway dividers, but if you travel back this way in the future, look to enjoy the **Laurel Hill Chute Trail**, the small trailhead for which is located between mileposts 50 and 51 on Hwy 26 eastbound. (You'll find it at the large Historical Marker sign, immediately after a long guardrail ends.) From the trailhead, you'll ascend a long set of stone steps and then head right on a section of the old paved State Hwy 26, where you'll soon come to the base of the dramatic upper section of the Laurel Hill chute on your left, complete with an interpretive sign. A trail leading up to the right will take you on a loop above the chute, and if you continue hiking along the old paved highway, you'll see another trail leading off to your left, which also leads back to the top of the Laurel Hill chute. Note that hiking along the old highway (Photo) until it terminates at a roadcut for Highway 26 in approximately 1.5 miles makes for an interesting hike, as well.

☐ **Next Sight:** Silent Rock

You won't be stopping at Silent Rock, but you would be wise to heed its legend.

During your descent of Mt. Hood on Hwy 26, you'll pass through a large roadcut approximately 4.5 miles west of Government Camp, and on the south side of the roadcut sits Silent Rock. Legend has it that all travelers passing Silent Rock *must* remain perfectly quiet as they pass so as to not incur bad luck. This means you must stop *all* conversations and turn off all devices, including your radio, iPhones, ear buds, etc. Skiers heading up to Mt. Hood for a day on the slopes know that if they remain quiet while passing Silent Rock, they will have an excellent day on the mountain. If they don't, then their day may turn epic. "Respect the rock!"

☐ **Next Stop:** Little Zig Zag Falls

It's hard to decide what is more picturesque, Little Zig Zag Falls itself or Little Zig Zag Creek leading up to it. (OK...down from it.) From the trailhead, follow this wide family-friendly trail through a shady forest and along the creek for perhaps 15 minutes to find Little Zig Zag Falls tumbling down as a cascade into a pool below. This is a somewhat quick stop with a very nice reward, especially on a warm summer day.

Driving Directions: Travel west on Hwy 26 from Government Camp for a little more than 4.5 miles to Kiwanis Camp Road /

Road 39, which is on your right just as Hwy 26 finishes its descent through a set of curves and begins a long straight stretch heading west. Turn right here and follow Kiwanis Camp Road for a little over 2 miles to where it ends at the trailhead for Little Zig Zag Falls. Park here and follow the obvious trail.

☐ **Next Stop:** More of Old State Highway 26

If Kiwanis Camp Road looks familiar, it's because it is another section of the old State Hwy 26, which you walked over when hiking along the Barlow Road Trail earlier today, and if you look carefully you'll see that the trailhead for Little Zig Zag Falls is located on a large bend in the old highway. After visiting Little Zig Zag Falls, you'll want to cross the old bridge found at the trailhead and follow old State Hwy 26 as it curves off through the forest to the southwest. In a short distance, you'll see on your right a small split rail fence, which marks a trail leading down the side of the old highway. Pass through this fence and follow the trail down to a tunnel below. Larger than necessary for people, yet too small for cars, this tunnel was built to accommodate riders on horseback making their way to and from Government Camp. By the way, the trail you're on here connects to the trail you were on earlier today, and is part of **Pioneer Bridal Trail**, a fun yet challenging mountain biking trail that descends all the way from Timberline Lodge to Rhododendron. For more information about this, visit MtHoodExpress.com

☐ **Next Stop:** Historic Barlow Road Tollgate

Along your journey west on Hwy 26, you'll pass a replica of the westernmost tollgate for the Barlow Road. Representing the last of five tollgates on the road, this replica is a nod to the original gate, which operated here from 1883 to 1918.

Driving Directions: You'll find the parking area for the historic Barlow Road Tollgate site 3.5 miles *west* of where you got back onto Hwy 26 from Kiwanis Camp Road / Road 39, or approximately ½ mile *east* of Rhododendron. The parking area is marked with a small sign that reads *Pioneer Bridal Trailhead.*

☐ **Next Stop:** Joe's Donut Shop

In the town of Sandy is Joe's Donut Shop, offering baked treats that have become an Oregon tradition. Long a "must stop" for skiers, campers, fishermen and anybody else spending time on Mt. Hood, Joe's is a "donut paradise" offering over 20 different varieties of fresh-baked donuts seven days a week.

Joe's Donut Shop
39230 Pioneer Blvd.
Sandy, OR 97055
503-668-7215

- 4:00 a.m. - 5:00 p.m. Monday - Friday
- 5:00 a.m. - 5:00 p.m. Saturdays and Sundays

☐ **Next Stop:** Sandy Historical Society Museum

The Sandy Historical Society Museum showcases the rich cultural and natural history of Mt. Hood and the surrounding area through captivating artifacts, displays and exhibits, as well as a classic Monty Python song! Be sure to stop in to catch the tune, explore the displays, and peruse the museum's extensive collection of fascinating books by local authors.

Sandy Historical Society Museum
39345 Pioneer Blvd.
Sandy, OR 97055

- 10:00 a.m. - 4:00 p.m. Monday - Saturday
- 12:00 p.m. - 4:00 p.m. Sunday

☐ **Last Stop:** Jonsrud Viewpoint

Your Mt. Hood road trip appropriately ends with an amazing view of Mt. Hood from the Jonsrud Viewpoint. With the Sandy River winding through the forest far below, this quaint stone viewpoint offers one of the finest views of majestic Mt. Hood you'll find from the west.

Driving Directions: As you reach the west end of "downtown" Sandy, turn right onto Bluff Road / Mt. Hood Scenic Byway. You'll find the viewpoint on your right at just under one mile.

Jonsrud Viewpoint
15652 Bluff Road
Sandy, OR 97055

☐ **Lunch Stop:** Tollgate Inn Restaurant & Bakery

If it's time for lunch, then consider a stop at Sandy's popular Tollgate Inn. Comprised of a collection of different buildings, all with an old-west theme, the Tollgate Inn offers classic American fare, with BBQ offerings, Chicken Pot Pie, Yankee Post Roast, burgers, classic sandwiches, hand cut steaks, and much more. Stop into the Bakery to enjoy scratch made pastries, made-to-order deli sandwiches, muffins, pies, cakes, and chocolates. Then grab an espresso, coffee or hot chocolate to enjoy while perusing the unique and intriguing gifts in their gift shop.

Tollgate Inn Restaurant & Bakery
38100 Hwy 26
Sandy, OR 97055
503-668-8456

Your Road Trip is Finished!

The Summit Ridge of 11,245' Mt. Hood - Photo: Mike Westby

Thank you for choosing to use our book during your road trip around Mt. Hood, and don't forget to email us a photo or two of your travels to **ContactUs@Discover-Oregon.com.** We'd love to see your shots and hear about your trip!

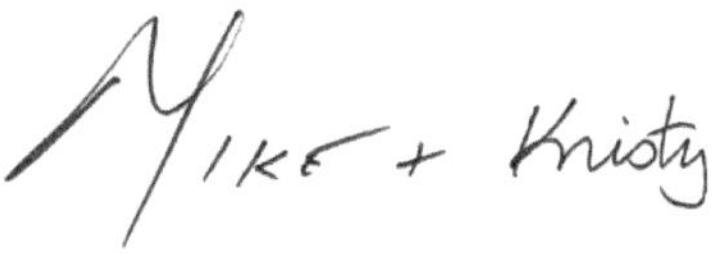

Leaving a Review

Can you do us a big favor? We'd like to ask you to leave a review of our book online, either on the web site through which you bought the book or another travel web site of your choosing. With the way online reviews work, a positive review goes *a long way* in helping to ensure we can continue to create and publish additional road trip titles. Thank you!

Phone Numbers Oregon Road Trips - Mt. Hood Edition
With the Columbia River Gorge

- Balch Hotel: 541-467-2277
- Biplane Flight – TacAero: 844-359-2827
- Bonneville Dam Interpretive Center: 541-374-8820
- Cloud Cap Inn Tour Reservations: 541-352-6002
- Columbia Gorge Discovery Center: 541-296-8600
- Columbia Gorge Hotel: 541-386-5566
- Columbia Gorge Hotel Spa: 541-387-8451
- Columbia Gorge Interpretive Center: 509-427-8211
- Columbia River Sternwheeler: 503-224-3900
- The Dalles Dam Tour & Visitor Center: 541-296-9778
- Hood River Hotel: 541-386-1900
- Hood River Ranger District: 541-352-6002
- Les Schwab Tire Center – Hood River: 541-386-1123
- Les Schwab Tire Center – Sandy: 503-668-3233
- Les Schwab Tire Center – The Dalles: 541-296-6134
- Mt. Hood Adventure Park at Skibowl: 503-272-3206
- Nichols Art Glass: 541-296-2143
- Oak Street Hotel: 541-386-3845
- Oregon Department of Transportation – 800-977-6368
- Oregon State Parks Parking Permit: 800-551-6949
- Timberline Lodge: 503-272-3311
- Timberline Lodge – Cascade Dining Room Reservations – 503-272-3311

US Army Corps of Engineers®
Portland District

AVERAGE MONTHLY FISH COUNT AT BONNEVILLE DAM

Here are the average monthly fish counts of common adult fish that pass Bonneville Lock and Dam. These fish are unique because they are anadromous (they begin their lives in fresh water, spend part of their life in the ocean, and return to fresh water to spawn). The majority of fish migrating upstream past Bonneville do so between March and November each year. The following numbers represent the ten year monthly average from 2006-2015.

Month	CHINOOK* SALMON (KING)	SOCKEYE SALMON (BLUEBACK)	COHO* SALMON (SILVER)	STEELHEAD TROUT	SHAD	LAMPREY
January	1	0	0	543	0	0
February	3	0	0	387	0	0
March	363	0	0	1,479	0	0
April	54,569	0	0	1,361	0	0
May	116,352	84	0	1,727	240,876	787
June	79,770	193,212	0	9,502	1,907,935	5,133
July	37,564	91,374	2	87,796	113,624	10,706
August	111,089	442	10,266	154,124	272	4,386
September	429,914	13	71,599	76,994	0	1,190
October	43,332	0	46,645	10,874	0	64
November	2,117	0	5,466	1,937	0	19
December	53	0	183	779	0	1

* Jacks included

THE HISTORIC COLUMBIA RIVER HIGHWAY

As you begin your Mt. Hood road trip, you will be traveling the "King of Roads", the Historic Columbia River Highway.

Built by eccentric railroad lawyer and entrepreneur Sam Hill and engineer Samuel Lancaster from 1913 to 1922, and modeled after Switzerland's Axenstrasse roadway around Lake Lucerne, the Historic Columbia River Highway stretches for nearly 75 miles from Troutdale to The Dalles, passing amidst the green maples, brightly colored moss and lush ferns of the Columbia River Gorge's western end before transitioning to the Ponderosa Pines and small oak trees dotting the semi-arid plateaus and hillsides of its eastern end. Along the way, this "great scenic boulevard", built for the Model Ts of its era, reveals a road that is an artistic masterpiece, showcasing retaining walls, guard rails, and structures master crafted from hand-hewn stone, logs and timbers. Connecting it all is a collection of graceful bridges that allow travelers to continue on their journey past stunning vistas and majestic waterfalls, with names like Latourell, Wahkeena, and Oneonta, as they make their way around, down, over and even through towering basalt cliffs toward their destination.

Though initially dedicated in 1916, the road began to pass into another era when construction on the I-84 freeway began in the 1930s. To make room for the new freeway, portions of the now "old" Columbia River Highway were blasted away, and tunnels through the basalt cliffs were either filled in or demolished. Today, however, portions of the Columbia River Highway are being restored. The Mosier Tunnels have been cleared of fill and are now open to cyclists and pedestrians, cyclists can ride from Troutdale to Cascade Locks, and the final segments of the Historic Columbia River Highway State Trail are being finished, thus allowing travelers to soon traverse from Troutdale all the way to The Dalles on the old highway or on newly restored portions closed to cars.

To learn more about Sam Hill, Samuel Lancaster, and the construction of the Historic Columbia River Highway, we highly recommend the book *Building the Columbia River Highway - They Said It Couldn't Be Done* by Peg Willis. You may want to pick up a copy and read it before you begin your journey. You'll be glad you did!

Off to Mt. Hood

The drive from Portland to Government Camp takes less than two hours today, but in the early 1900s such a journey required three days of arduous travel over dirt roads that would turn to deep mud with just a good rainstorm. The book *Off to Mt. Hood* shares the fascinating personal accounts of Ivan M. Wooley, a young tour guide who ferried guests up and down the mountain in a "modern" 1907 Pierce Arrow.

The 1937 Steiner Church

"A Premier Oregon Historical Destination"

During the years of 1925 through 1952, Henry Steiner, along with his wife Mollie, two sons John and Fred, and 11 other children, built 100 log cabins and two log churches in the forests at the base of majestic Mt. Hood. Not your typical log structures, instead each was built by hand using only logs, branches, river stones, and other materials all gleaned from the forest surrounding each building site, with many pieces chosen for a quirky bent shape, a fancy burl, an oddly split trunk, a dramatic twist in a branch or other whimsical characteristic. As a result, every structure Henry Steiner built was filled with unique architectural features and details, all of which gave them their signature "Steiner" look. Today, each of these log structures is a highly-prized

and revered story element in Oregon's rich history, with the 1937 Steiner Church being the crown jewel in the collection.

While the 1937 Steiner Church no longer holds services, it is now open to the public for self-guided tours on the first Saturday of every month, from 10:00 a.m. to 4:00 p.m.

You'll find the 1937 Steiner Church a few miles west of Rhododendron, Oregon, in the town of Welches, Oregon, just off of Hwy 26. If your road trip brings you through Welches during the 1937 Steiner Church's operating hours on the first Saturday of every month, then by all means you'll want to stop in and tour this "must see" historical destination. If your road trip does not occur during the church's operating hours, then make plans to return to see this beautiful architectural wonder. Note that groups of four or more can make reservations to tour the church at any time. Admission is required.

To learn more and to see many additional photos, visit www.SteinerChurch.com

The 1937 Steiner Church
68835 E. Barlow Trail Rd.
Welches, OR 97067
www.SteinerChurch.com

Now Enjoy An Oregon Coast Road Trip!

Oregon Road Trips - Oregon Coast Edition

Explore the grandeur of Oregon's dramatic coastline during an adventurous 3 to 9-day road trip from Astoria south to Brookings. You'll journey along Oregon's beautiful Highway 101 as you discover countless scenic beaches, tour historic lighthouses, wander through quaint beach towns, watch whales spouting just off shore, ride in the cab of a 1925 steam locomotive, eat tasty Dungeness Crab fresh off the boat...or catch your own, stay in historic hotels, explore unique shops, meet friendly people and so much more. Best of all...everything is already planned for you!

Your perfect Oregon Coast road trip awaits!

Available Now at Retailers Throughout Oregon, Discover-Oregon.com, and Online

And Another Great Road Trip is Ready!

Oregon Road Trips - Southeast Edition

If you enjoyed this Mt. Hood road trip, then you're sure to enjoy exploring remote Southeast Oregon. As with this title, you'll simply turn each page as you motor along and choose which points of interest to stop at and explore during your day's journey, *all while making your way toward that evening's lodging in a historic Oregon hotel.*

You'll drive to the top of 9,734' Steens Mountain, stay in the 1923 Frenchglen Hotel, explore the remote Leslie Gulch, see how stage coaches are built, dig for fossils, hike "Crack in the Ground", look for wild Mustangs, eat at a truly unique and remote Oregon restaurant, marvel at the geologic wonders of the Journey Through Time Scenic Byway and so much more!

Available Now at Retailers Throughout Oregon, Discover-Oregon.com, and Online

SOUTHWEST OREGON AWAITS!

Oregon Road Trips - Southwest Edition

Visit 13 historic covered bridges, spend a night in Crater Lake Lodge, discover a vintage aircraft museum, enjoy a play in Ashland, explore deep into the Oregon Caves, wander an Oregon ghost town, see some of Oregon's most beautiful waterfalls, tour the Applegate Wine Trail, and so much more on your 9-day road trip through Southwest Oregon. As with our other Oregon Road Trip books, you'll simply motor along while you discover Oregon, and finish each night at a unique historic hotel!

Your Southwest Oregon road trip awaits, and it's already planned for you!

Available Now at Retailers Throughout Oregon, Discover-Oregon.com, and Online

What to See, Do & Explore on the Oregon Coast!

At 363 miles long, Oregon's scenic coastline is filled with countless natural wonders and attractions to see, do, and explore. Hike to a high bluff to watch for whales, walk a long sandy beach, explore a historic lighthouse, catch a live Dungeness crab, join in the fun of a sandcastle building contest, even ride aboard an old-fashioned steam train. The problem is...how do you uncover all of these activities to get the most out of your trip? The solution is the new *Oregon Coast Guide*. Inside these pages, you'll discover **over 300** fun and adventurous things to see, do and explore while visiting the Oregon Coast, complete with descriptions, photos, maps, tips, a whale watching guide and much more.

Available Now at Retailers Throughout Oregon, Discover-Oregon.com, and Online

Explore the Columbia River Gorge

Cutting a deep gorge between Oregon and Washington, the majestic Columbia River Gorge is filled with scenic vistas, graceful waterfalls, amazing attractions, captivating history, and countless adventures, and they are all waiting for you in the *Columbia River Gorge - An Explorer's Guide.* With this guide you'll discover the beautiful waterfalls of the "Waterfall Corridor", walk among the gorge's colorful spring wildflowers, fly in a vintage 2-seater biplane over Mt. Hood, see over 300 restored antique motorcars and aeroplanes up close, explore the Hood River "Fruit Loop", hike classic gorge trails, visit Oregon's oldest bookstore, discover some great new cycling roads and routes, watch world-class sailboarding, see giraffes, zebras, camels, and bison, stay a night or two or three at one of the gorge's historic hotels, watch a master glass blower create a stunning trout out of glass, eat the biggest ice cream cone in your life, and so much more. **Over 150 things in all!**

Available Now at Retailers Throughout Oregon, Discover-Oregon.com, and Online

Explore Washington's Olympic Peninsula

Now easily discover **over 150** things to see, do and explore on Washington's Northern Olympic Peninsula!

The majestic northern Olympic Peninsula is filled with scenic vistas, beautiful beaches, graceful waterfalls, amazing attractions, and countless adventures, and they're all waiting for you in the *Northern Olympic Peninsula - An Explorer's Guide*. Tour a vintage aeroplane museum, visit historic lighthouses, learn how wooden kayaks are made, sleep in your very own castle, see Orcas, Gray Whales, and Humpbacks up close, discover the most beautiful waterfall on the Olympic Peninsula, explore historic Fort Worden, hike stunning Shi Shi and Rialto beaches, hike the captivating Hoh Rainforest, wander old town Port Townsend, and so much more!

Available Now at Retailers
Throughout Washington and Online

Oregon & 1

Oregon, we want to start a grass roots movement.

Imagine if every business in Oregon, large or small, huge or tiny, promoted *at least* one other Oregon business...at no charge, which is completely unrelated to their business.

- A small café promotes a bookstore on its menu.
- A bookstore promotes a historical carousel with a placard by the cash register.
- A historical carousel promotes a tour provider with a small sign near the ticket counter.
- A tour provider promotes a tire store with a mention on its brochures.
- A tire store promotes a local hotel with a note on its invoices.
- A local hotel promotes a theater in the next town over with current showtimes listed at its check-in counter.
- A local theater promotes an auto repair shop with a small sign on its door.
- An auto repair shop promotes a small café with a menu placed in the waiting room.

Creative opportunities to promote Oregon businesses are endless. Better yet, each requires *very little effort or expense* and can start right now...at your business. How do you decide who to promote? Let your employees pick their favorites and rotate their choices on a regular basis.

With all of us extending a hand to our fellow Oregonians beginning today, we can build a powerful interconnected web that reaches all across the state and cross-promotes thousands and thousands of Oregon businesses every day, thus lifting our state's economy, adding to your neighbor's paycheck, and bringing more business to your business.

Oregon and 1!

WE RECOMMEND OREGON SMALL BUSINESSES...

Building The Columbia River Highway

The intriguing story of how visionary artists, poets and engineers came together to forge a route through the mighty Columbia River Gorge and create the nation's first scenic highway, a "poem in stone." Ride along with author Peg Willis as she explores the beginnings of this miracle highway, the men who created it, and the obstacles they overcame on the road to its completion.

Mt. Hood - Adventures of the Wy'East Climbers

A *fascinating* read about the intrepid climbers of the Golden Era on Mt. Hood, the 1930s. Learn all about those who dared to forge first ascents, battled the elements to rescue fellow climbers, and manned the lookout atop Mt. Hood's lofty and often violent summit. Available online, as well as at the Mt. Hood Cultural Center & Museum in Government Camp.

Les Schwab Tire Centers

If you're on the road and have a flat tire, brake issues or a similar problem, we highly recommend the very helpful folks at your nearby Les Schwab Tire Center. You'll find locations in Hood River, OR, The Dalles, OR, and Sandy, OR. Their phone numbers are listed on Page 128.

75 Classic Rides: Oregon

From an after-work ride through Portland's neighborhood streets or a family cycle along the flat Willamette Valley Scenic Bikeway, to a multi-day tour in the salty breezes of the Oregon coast—if you're seeking the best bike trails in Oregon, you'll find plenty of blacktop bliss in Jim Moore's *75 Classic Rides: Oregon.*

Antiques & Oddities

A Columbia River Gorge "destination" for over 20 years, Antiques & Oddities in Bingen, WA is home to an eclectic collection of quality antiques from near and far, including Asia and Europe. Stop in when you're in the Gorge, and be sure to make your way downstairs to check out their latest arrivals.

211 W. Steuben St.
Bingen, WA 98605
509-493-4242

Camp Attitude

"Changing lives one camper at a time!"

Camp Attitude provides a welcoming camp experience for disabled youth and their families. Here, children with special needs can participate in all of the fun, games, excitement and interaction of a thrilling week-long "summer camp" experience, all for a nominal fee, thanks to donations from contributors who enjoy seeing a smile on a child's face...and a squirt gun in their hand!

Camp Attitude is a faith-based non-profit organization, and donations may be made by visiting their web site at www.CampAttitude.org

Camp Attitude
PO Box 2017
45829 S Santiam Hwy
Foster, OR 97345
541-401-1052

ARE YOU A DISNEY FAN?

In addition to our popular Oregon and Washington Road Trip and regional guidebooks, Deschutes River Press also publishes three books about Disney history and the theme parks.

Disney History - Rare & Unknown

Over 55 articles, complete with more than 175 color photos, take you on a magical journey where you'll discover rare and unknown story elements of Disney history, many of which are published here for the very first time!

Available online, as well as at the prestigious Walt Disney Family Museum and the Walt Disney Hometown Museum.

The Hidden Secrets & Stories of Disneyland

Enjoy a fascinating and entertaining book that reveals over 250 of the hidden secrets and story elements which the Disney Imagineers have purposely hidden for Disneyland guests to discover and enjoy, complete with 225 photos!

Available online, as well as at the prestigious Walt Disney Family Museum, the Walt Disney Boyhood Home, and the Walt Disney Hometown Museum.

Made in United States
Troutdale, OR
02/03/2025

28610968R00086